Glance Gaylord

Gilbert's Last Summer at Rainford

And What it Taught Him

Glance Gaylord

Gilbert's Last Summer at Rainford
And What it Taught Him

ISBN/EAN: 9783744694339

Printed in Europe, USA, Canada, Australia, Japan

Cover: Foto ©Thomas Meinert / pixelio.de

More available books at **www.hansebooks.com**

GILBERT'S LAST SUMMER AT RAINFORD,

AND

WHAT IT TAUGHT..

BY
GLANCE GAYLORD,
AUTHOR OF "BOY'S AT DR. MURRAY'S,"
"GILBERT STARR," &C.

———

BOSTON:
GRAVES & YOUNG,
1867.

RAINFORD SERIES.

VOL. I.—GILBERT STARR AND HIS LESSONS.

" II.—GILBERT'S LAST SUMMER AT RAINFORD.

OTHER VOLUMES IN PRESS.

Contents.

CHAPTER I.
ON THE ICE, ... 9

CHAPTER II.
A LITTLE BOY'S COURAGE, ... 28

CHAPTER III.
PLOTTING, ... 43

CHAPTER IV.
GILBERT'S DISMAY, ... 61

CHAPTER V.
AN UNKNOWN FRIEND, ... 78

CHAPTER VI.
GATES'S DISMAY, ... 95

CHAPTER VII.
VERY PLEASANT DAYS, ... 115

CHAPTER VIII.
FEAR COMETH AS DESOLATION, ... 131

CHAPTER IX.
GILBERT'S OFFER, ... 150

viii   CONTENTS.

CHAPTER X.
THE SHADOW OF DEATH, ... 158

CHAPTER XI.
GRIEVING FOR TWO, ... 185

CHAPTER XII.
"O RAY!" 203

CHAPTER XIII.
WHAT FOLLOWED A TUMBLE, ... 221

CHAPTER XIV.
GILBERT'S AWAKENING, , ... 237

CHAPTER XV.
"THE POOR OLD CAPTAIN," 255

CHAPTER XVI.
MOSTLY ABOUT LETTERS, ... 275

CHAPTER XVII.
DID THE SUMMER TEACH ANYTHING? . . 292

CHAPTER XVIII.
FAREWELLS, ... 314

Gilbert's Last Summer at Rainford.

CHAPTER I.

ON THE ICE.

IT was a clear, crisp, sparkling night; the
sky fairly white with stars, and the glit-
tering crescent of a new moon dipping behind the roofs on Riverside hill. · Winter was
drawing to a close, though you would not
have suspected it, had you seen how hard
the river was frozen, — from the foot of Mr.
Winterhalter's lawn, quite across to the
wharves and boat-houses on the other side,
and felt the keen air, and heard the ring —
of the skaters' steel, and their shouts and

echoing laughter. Now, although it was actually the first of March, and time for sunnier skies and balmier ˜winds, there was not a boy in Mr. Winterhalter's school, or Professor Roth's, as for that matter, who did not rejoice at the sudden cold snap which this first spring month brought.

There had been a great dearth of skating all winter, — "not enough to keep our skates bright," Tom Fowler said, — and now that it had actually come, real, genuine skating, there was great excitement and much joy about the matter. So, on this clear, calm, brilliant night, Mr. Winterhalter's boys and the Professor's were all on the river, and a merry time of it they were having. There were the under and upper classes, and boys of all sizes, from Forrest, the head-boy of the Professor's school, down to little Ned Rogers, the smallest boy in Mr. Winterhalter's establishment, and who was generally

under everybody's feet, and being knocked
down and picked up continually.

Now, if you have not a poor memory, you
will remember that Gilbert Starr had been
deprived of the captaincy of the Boat Club,
and had been "cut" by all his friends and
comrades, save Ray Hunter and Perry Kent,
for doing what he thought to be his duty.
You will remember, too, that though his old
comrades and friends, who had been under his
command, discovered he was not a sham like
some of themselves, but honest and manly
and true, yet they were too proud and stub-
born to acknowledge this, and passed Gilbert
by in all their plans, and would have nothing
to do with him. The winter had worn thus
far away, and, so far as Gilbert and his men
were concerned, matters had not mended a
bit. They never spoke to him, nor took the
slightest heed of his going or coming; and
though they *did* secretly admire and respect

him very much, they allowed nothing of this
to be seen, and followed the instructions of
their new captain, Philip Gates, very obedi-
ently, considering what an overbearing fellow Gates was. Captain Philip was very
bitter toward Gilbert for many reasons. In
the first place, Gilbert was still head-boy, and
kept to his books so faithfully that Gates,
who cared little for study, could not displace
him and take the position himself. In the
second place, he knew that Gilbert stood a
long way above him, so far as manliness and
courage and honesty were concerned, and he
knew that his own men knew it; and when
a person is conscious of this superiority in
one whom he has wronged, the knowledge
is apt to make him very bitter and jeal-
ous and vengeful. At least this was the
case with Gates, and it caused him to be-
have toward Gilbert in a manner very shame-
ful for a boy who made any pretence to

honor or honesty. He ·slandered his rival,
he told many falsehoods_ about him to his class,
in order to keep them as much estranged
from Gilbert as possible, and he was not at
all above annoying the ex-captain with mean
and petty tricks. Ray Hunter, Gilbert's
faithful friend, had partly rebelled from
Gates's authority, and no one was quite sure
whether he belonged to the Boat Club or not.
And thus matters stood on this starry winter
night, when they were all gathered on the
river.

It was a most perfect night for skating, —
very keen and biting, it was true, but without a breath of wind. In the middle of the
river they had a great bonfire, that sent
broad pathways of light far up and down the
ice ; and besides the school-boys, there were
plenty of the Rainford town-people out to
see and enjoy the sport.

Colored lanterns gleamed and flickered a

along the river-side, and shot and zig-zagged
across the ice, suspended from some skater's
arm, and what with their gay gleaming, and
the merry, boisterous groups of skaters, and
the roaring and crackling of the fire that
floated red sparks up into the night, the
scene was as bright and vivid as heart could
wish.   Now Captain Philip Gates was exceedingly self-satisfied and light of heart this
evening, being a very good skater, and having already beaten several of his men in
racing.   He was very anxious to have a race
between his men and Captain Forrest's, of
the Professor's school.   He flew about from
one place to another, getting his men together, and talking with Forrest's about the
matter.   Of course they were ready enough
for the trial of speed, and soon both of the
clubs were around the fire, clamoring and
discussing the point of departure.   But Captain Forrest was absent, and as his men

thought they could do nothing without him,
Gates started off in search of him, after waiting impatiently some minutes for his arrival.

After searching long and diligently among
the crowd within light of the fire, Captain
Gates decided that Forrest was not there,
and began to cruise about along the riverside, where there were many solitary figures
as well as gay skating parties. After pur-
suing several fleeting figures, to find that
they were quite other persons than Forrest,
he gave up the search on Mr. Winterhalter's
side of the river, and crossed over to Riverside. Here the river lay quite dark in the
shadow of the great hill, and the skaters were
few and far between; only now and then he
stumbled upon some unfortunate individual,
who was making a first attempt at skating,
and preferred to hide his falls and clumsiness
in the darkness, and speeding on, till he was
half in despair of finding the object of his

search, he came at last to where he caught
the echo of two pairs of skates a long way
before him, neither of them moving very
fast, but smoothly and glibly, as if their
owners' found it the easiest thing in the
world to do. "One of those pairs of feet
belong to Forrest," thought Gates, increasing
his speed, "but whose can the other be?"
The skaters changed their course a little
after that, and turned toward the opposite
bank of the river, and as they moved only
leisurely, Gates was soon near them. On
they moved, across the wide path of light
which the bonfire cast up the river, and then
Gates discovered, with a thrill of chagrin
and disappointment, that Forrest's companion was Gilbert Starr. "Pshaw!" he exclaimed angrily, "what are he and Forrest
together for, and at the very moment when
I don't want Starr around?" He slackened
his pace, considering how he should call For-

rest away; and then, fearful that he should lose sight of them altogether among the merry crowd which was setting that way, he came up behind them as noiselessly as possible, just in time to hear Forrest say, as he put his hand on Gilbert's shoulder, "We were talking about the fight, you know; or rather about how we tried to fight, and Perry Kent brought Mr. Winterhalter down upon us. I've laughed about that affair a hundred times since! I don't know but it was the best thing that could have happened, for it made us friends—you see, and that's a great deal, I think."

"I was very hot and quick, that time," said Gilbert, as they glided along, "and I really didn't treat Mr. Prescott civilly. But I apologized; I asked his forgiveness!"

"Trust you for that!" said Forrest; "but I was thinking what a droll affair the whole of it was; and looking back I think, well. I think

I admire you more and more every day for the stand you took against what you thought was wrong. I only wish *I* could have done it! Though," added Forrest, "I don't think I ever could give up my captainship, especially if I knew such a fellow as that Gates was to take my place."

Captain Philip fell back a little at hearing this, biting his lips very hard, yet keeping near enough to hear Gilbert answer, "Well, I did find it hard, very hard; but I came through it; and as for Gates, — well, I've nothing to say about Gates, anyway."

"Nothing to say about me, eh!" said Captain Philip to himself, as he stealthily followed. "Oh, you confounded Gilbert Starr! Oh! you hateful scamp! I wish the ice would open and let you in, confound you!" But the ice did not open, and the two figures before him glided smoothly on, and Gates followed them in their windings among the

crowd, prevented, now, however, from hearing what they were talking about; and pretty quick one of Forrest's men spied his captain, as the two drew near the fire.

" Here, Captain!" he cried out, " we want
you! Gates is looking everywhere for you,
and we want to race. Where *have* you
been?"

"Taking a turn or two on our side of the
river," said Forrest; "and if you want to
race, go ahead. I don't object, I'm sure."

" But we want you to head us," said his
men, gathering about him. " Gates is going
to lead his men, and we want you to lead
us."

Just then Captain Gates came sailing up
to the group, saying, very innocently,

" Oh, here you are, Forrest! I've been
looking everywhere for you. What do you
say to the race? "

" I don't object," said Forrest, rather coldly, leaning one arm upon Gilbert's shoulder.

"Then let's get at it, right off," said Gates, briskly, while he looked at his watch; "it's half-past eight, already, and we'll have to go in at nine, I suppose."

"Yes, nine to a minute, Winterhalter said," said Tom Fowler.

Forrest's men began to clamor around him, threatening that they would not race unless he headed them.

"Very well," said he, at last; "I'll go, just to please you. Scatter!"

Then he turned to Gilbert. "It's a shame," he said, indignantly; "you're shut out of every thing. I've a good mind to stay with you, and not go a step!"

"Oh, no!" said Gilbert; "I don't mind, — that is, not much. I'm getting used to it, you see."

Forrest shook his head. "A fellow can't do that,—not entirely," he said; "but you're made of different stuff than I, somehow. You don't mind what would kill me. But they're calling, and I must go. Good-night, Starr, if I don't see you again," he called back over his shoulder, as he glided off to his men.

Gilbert stood by the fire, and watched them all go scurrying down the river into the darkness, thinking that Forrest was a very good-hearted fellow indeed, and feeling very glad of his friendship. " And," he thought to himself, " it was only such a very little while ago that we were under the Rain- ford bridge fighting for the *honor* of our schools ! What days those were ! "

They seemed a long way off, somehow, after all; so much had happened between those days and these. " All this long winter," he said to himself, " my men have hated me and shunned me, and oh ! I wonder if all this is never going to end ? Mrs. Winterhal- ter says, ' Yes ! ' but the end is a dreadfully long time coming. I'm to leave school next

fall, and though I don't care so much about
the captaincy, I wouldn't like to leave with
the fellows all hating me. I'd like to be
friends with 'em, anyhow."

Some one came gliding around the fire,
and thrust his hands into Gilbert's. It was
his protege, Perry Kent. "Well," said Gilbert, his face brightening at the sight of the
boy, "have you skated enough for one
night?"

"Not half," said Perry; "and I wish
you'd come down the river a bit with me.
It's as smooth as glass down there, and Ray
and all the rest are down there racing."

"What's that to me?" said Gilbert, a little
bitterly, "since there's not one of 'em
that cares where I am. But, pshaw!" he
quickly added, "I believe I'm getting blue
and gloomy. I'll go! Come, Perry!" and
taking the boy's hands, he sped away back-
ward, drawing his protege swiftly after him.

They went like the wind. The fire shrank away behind them into the distance, till it looked like a round fiery eye. Gilbert whirled away towards the Riverside shore, where the ice was silent and deserted. Sometimes, above the ringing of their own steel, they caught the echo of the boys' shouts far below. Releasing Perry, he spun round and round in dizzy circles, still bearing downward all the time, and suddenly, before there was a breath in which to think of danger, Gilbert went through with a great crash, and the little boy was standing there — alone.

Terror and dismay froze the cry for help that was on his lips. He looked up at the great red eye gleaming down the river-way, with a vague consciousness that there lay help and succor. But still he did not cry out, nor stir from the spot where he had stopped. There came to his ears a faint sound of crashing and crackling of brittle fragments from the darkness, a little way to his right, and the sound brought suddenly back his senses, and a warm thrill ran through every vein of his body, and before another minute had elapsed, he was at the edge of the great yawning hole in the ice, crying, "Gilbert! Gilbert!"

"Yes," said Gilbert from out the darkness, and Perry could hear him clutch at the edges of the ice, and hear the fearful sound of the brittle fragments crumbling and giving away.

"Oh, Gilbert!" cried the boy, "what shall I do?"

It seemed a fearful length of time before Gilbert answered, though in reality it was only a few seconds, and then he only said, "I don't know. It's a long way to — to help!"

Perry looked up to where the fire shone,

and realized this with a shiver of anguish.
If he went so far for help, he was terribly
afraid that Gilbert would not be there when
he returned. He did not ask Gilbert's advice again, but groped his way around the
yawning hole to the point which he fancied
was nearest him. And before Gilbert suspected Perry's intention, he suddenly felt the
boy's hands upon his shoulders, clasping him
with all the strength of which they were ca-
pable.

"I'll never let go! I'll never let go!"
Perry cried with a trembling voice; "but
O, Gilbert, tell me what to do!"

In spite of his peril, and the awful cold
that was numbing him, Gilbert's old fore-
thought and regard did not desert him.

"No, Perry!" he said bravely, drawing
himself back as much as he dared, "let go of
me! let go of me, I tell you! You'll only
get yourself in."

Perry did let go, but it was only to get a fresh hold, and to twist his stout woollen tippet under Gilbert's arms. Then Gilbert felt him pulling back with all his strength, though the ice cracked and trembled warningly.

"Stop!" Gilbert commanded; "stop!"

But Perry took not the least heed of his injunctions, and fairly kept his friend afloat, while he shouted lustily. But who would mind a shout, when shouts and cries were echoing from all directions? The little boy's heart began to sink. It seemed as if his friend was sinking deeper and deeper.

"O, Gilbert!" said he, tremulously, "just speak to me."

Gilbert managed to chatter, "K-keep up g-g-good courage," but there was something in his tone that made Perry's heart sink yet lower, for it seemed just as if Gilbert had lost *his* courage. Then Gilbert spoke once more, brave and kind to the last.

"Perry," he said, "you — you're slipping n-n-nearer and nearer. Let go of me!"

"No! no!" said Perry, frantically, "never, Gilbert!"

The boy laid his ear to the ice, listened breathlessly, and waited. Such long, fearful seconds! with Gilbert in the very grasp of Death!—oh, *so* long! *so* long! But then it came — the sound for which he was listening — and in a second more he was sure of it, for their lanterns began to flare and flicker along the ice-path, and their shouts rang up the river, and the racers were returning. Something choked so in Perry's throat, that he could not speak for a moment, then he cried,

"Hold on! hold on a little longer, Gilbert! Help is coming — it's right here — and it's Ray, and Forrest and all of them! Hold on to me, Gilbert! — hold on!"

Up the river swept the skaters, joyously and boisterously.

CHAPTER II.

A LITTLE BOY'S COURAGE.

BUT now a new fear took possession of Perry's heart. He began to tremble lest the flying racers should pass by without heeding or noticing Gilbert's peril. They were coming at such speed, that he knew they would flash by in a twinkling, and if once they passed, all hope was gone. So he began to cry for help at the top of his voice, — shouting and screaming, and bidding Gilbert keep up good courage between his cries, — and up came the racers, their lanterns flaring great rays of light up and down and across the river, and one of them fell upon Gilbert's

28

white face. There was a look upon it that made Perry redouble his cries, and exclaim,

"O, Gilbert! just one minute more! only a minute!"

But in less than that time the skaters were abreast of them — they were almost past — when suddenly one who bore a light swerved out from the line, and giving a cry darted toward the spot where Perry was waiting in such trembling anxiety. Two or three of the skaters followed to see what was the matter, and the remainder swept on up the river, like the wind.

It was Ray Hunter who heard Perry's cry from out the darkness, and it was Captain Forrest and one of his men who followed. The lantern-light showed them what had happened before they could reach the edge of the air-hole into which Gilbert had fallen, and giving a great cry, Ray pressed forward with such headlong speed, that he came near going in, too.

" O, Gilbert ! " he exclaimed, " catch hold
of me — quick ! I can keep you up ! Catch
hold of me — quick ! quick ! "

But Gilbert was too thoroughly benumbed
for that, which Ray perceived and caught his
friend by the shoulder, while Forrest, with a
very white face, got down beside him, and
the two tried to pull Gilbert out. But the
ice cracked and crumbled, and both came
near pitching in headlong. Then Forrest
darted away, saying, " Hold him for a minute, Hunter, till I can get a rail," and with
that he vanished in the darkness.

Ray bent over Gilbert, clutching him firmly, and whispering, " O, Gilbert ! —don't give
up ! don't think of it ! I've got you, and you
can't go under. O ! how *did* you get in this
fix, old fellow, and how long have you been
here ? "

But Gilbert's teeth chattered so, that he
did not attempt to answer, and Ray's heart
seemed almost to stop its beating, Forrest

was gone so long! But he came in a few seconds after, dragging his burden behind him, and Ray said, " God bless you, Forrest, but hurry ! hurry ! "

There was no need of telling Forrest that. He pushed the rail across the gap, letting its ends rest on the firm and solid ice. Then he got astride of it, his feet thrust down into the water beside Gilbert's, and putting his arms under Gilbert's own, drew him up as far as his strength would allow, and here Ray and Forrest's man got hold and all together they drew Gilbert out on to the unyielding ice.

" There ! " said Forrest; " and now lean upon me, Starr, for you're too cold to stand alone. Don't mind, for I can bear you up; " and to prove it, he fairly lifted Gilbert off the ice. Ray was down upon his knees, and had his friend's skates off in a twinkling.

" Now," said he, " we must start for home

in an instant ! Can you ever stand it to get
there, old fellow? Forrest, you shall take
one shoulder, and I the other, — and, are you
ready ?"

Just then Gates and the rest came whirling back down the river, to see what had
taken Forrest and Ray, and this arrival hin-
dered them a little, there were so many questions to be answered. Now there was not
one of Gilbert's old men but what longed to
have a reconciliation then and there. Their
old captain had but just escaped a cold, cruel
death; and there is something in the near
approach of death and danger which is almost
always sure to soften the stubbornest heart,
and make it long for peace and reconciliation
with its fellow man. There were none of
Gilbert's men, but in whose hearts there was
a desire to take their old captain's hand, tell
him they were glad that he was safe, and
help him up to the house. But Gates fell

back as soon as he had made out all about the affair, and called his men to come away. They lingered, wavered, but finally obeyed.

"Oh," said Forrest, his voice full of scorn and indignation, "I'm glad that I haven't such a set of fellows under me.! I'd choose to run away from them if I had. Here, Fred and Wayne and Frank," he called to his men, "come and give us a hand, for the captain is fairly faint with cold. Come, all of you, and put those fellows to shame!"

They came, Forrest's whole command, and taking Gilbert carried him quickly toward home. They did not ·follow the river up, but struck across the snowy meadows in a direct line for Mr. Winterhalter's, and there were so many of them to help, that Gilbert was no burden at all. But, if you are a boy and have at all the same sensibilities that Gilbert had, you will know what a hard thing for him it was to be carried home by his old rival's men, while those who were rightly his own hung back, and did not seem to care that even his life had been saved. He said not a word till he found himself in the warm hall leading to the schoolroom, with Forrest and all his men about him, and Mrs. Winterhalter looking at him with a very frightened face.

"Why, Gilbert, what have you been about?" said she; "wet to the skin, and your clothes half-frozen to you!"

"I've been in the river," he chattered, "and I should have drowned but for Perry Kent."

"Perry Kent!" said Forrest; "where is he?"

Then there was a great search for Perry, who was at last found in the shadow of the doorway and brought forward to receive the praise and thanks which Ray and Forrest

and Mrs. Winterhalter and everybody were
ready to shower upon him. Forrest called
him a little hero, which was great praise
in the eyes of the rest of the boys, who
looked upon Forrest always with envy and
admiration, and Ray said, taking Perry's
hand before them all,—"I thought you
hadn't much courage, but I take all that
back. There's more to you than I thought,
and you can't know how much I thank you.
Thanks!—why, thanks are just nothing to
what I want to say!" and so he left everything else that he thought unsaid, and went
up stairs with Gilbert.

Mrs. Winterhalter pressed a great many
thanks upon Forrest, and said, among other
things, "I'm very glad indeed, that there's
such good feeling between you and our
head-boy. It's not much like the feeling
that was between you two last summer, my
dear?"

Forrest colored a little, but answered promptly, "No ma'am! but Gilbert and I are good friends now; I don't believe we could be better, and I admire him very much; and I *do* wish he could be captain again instead of that——, excuse me, Mrs. Winterhalter, but I *don't* like Gates!"

Mrs. Winterhalter smiled a little, but did not say whether that was her opinion, or no; only, "I tell Gilbert that that will all come right by-and-by, and I think he thinks so, too. Do you know," she said, laying her hand lightly on Forrest's shoulder, "that I think it often does a boy a great deal of good to go through such a trial as Gilbert is going through."

"It is very disagreeable, and very bothersome," said Forrest, "and I think *I* should break down under it, Mrs. Winterhalter."

"No, no," said she, brightly, "I hope not. But I think, and perhaps you've noticed it,

that Gilbert· is much firmer and stronger
for the right than he used to be, — without
losing the brightness and gayety that are so
natural to him, too, which is a great deal.
And if he can only persevere to the end I
have great hopes for him."

" He will ! — you may he sure of that ! "
said Forrest, quickly; " I never saw such a
fellow to persevere, no matter what any one
thinks or says of him. But if you'll let me,
I'd like to just run up and say good-night,
for I must go back right away. The Professor'll scold me finely now, I expect."

Mrs. Winterhalter gave him permission,
adding, — " The Professor will not be very
angry when he sees those drenched boots
and knows what you have been about."

The nine o'clock bell tinkled just as Forrest ran up stairs. " Whew ! " he said to
himself, " here it's nine o'clock and I ought
to be in my own bed across the river. But

it's not every night that a fellow comes near being drowned, as Starr has, and I guess the Professor'll excuse me. At any rate, I'll see him a minute."

He had been in the Boat Club's room once before, and so knew the way, and presently Ray was startled a little by seeing him enter.

" You, Forrest?" he exclaimed; " why, I thought you'd gone long ago."

" So do my men, I suppose, but that good Mrs. Winterhalter had a word to say to me, and I wanted to see Starr comfortable, and here I am! How are you, old fellow?" he asked, sitting down on the bed by Gilbert.

Gilbert still shivered and chattered in spite of the load of blankets that was on him, but was very grateful for Forrest's attention, and told him so.

" Pshaw!" said the Professor's head-boy, " it's nothing. You'd have done the same for me if I had chanced to need it, and a great deal more, I dare say. I know you."

"It was such a narrow escape!" said Ray, shuddering; "if Gilbert had been alone we never should have found him."

"We were not any to soon as it was," said Forrest; "however, a miss is as good as a mile, they say — though I'd rather have the mile — and I hope we'll see you out on the river in a night or two, Starr."

Gilbert did not make much of a reply; and just then Gates and his men came clattering up stairs to bed, and Forrest got up hastily, saying, "There come all the fellows, and I'll be going. I hate that Gates, by the way. And — good-night, Gilbert," coming back to shake the ex-captain's hand; and then he bent over and whispered, so that Ray might not hear, "Do you know — I'd like to do as you have done, as you are doing, my dear fellow! Will you help me?" and without waiting for an answer, or to see how Gilbert received it, he hurried away, meeting all

the Boat Club at the door. Their faces
showed how surprised they were at seeing
him there, and at that time of night, but
Forrest paid them very little attention and
passed on his homeward way. The boys
went to bed, stealing many glances at the.
bed where Gilbert lay, and longing, every
one of them, in their secret hearts, to go and
shake his hand and ask him how he did,—of
course excepting Gates.

Then the room began to grow still and
quiet, as the remainder of the house had
long been. Only Ray was up, waiting to
see whether Gilbert was going to get warm
or not. And presently he said, after he was
sure the boys were all asleep, "Isn't he a
nice fellow?—Forrest, I mean."

"Yes," said Gilbert in a very grateful
tone, "he's very good indeed to me, and I
like him very much."

"And think of Perry Kent! Why, you

know I always thought him weak and baby-
ish, for all you said that there was the real
grit in him. Now he's proved himself, and
I'm glad of it for his own sake as well as
yours. I think he'll rise a long way in the
boys' opinion."

"Yes," said Gilbert, "and I never shall
forget how his face looked for those few
minutes before you came in sight. The fire
way up the river shone on it a little, just
enough for me to see. Well," he added,
drawing a long breath of content, "it's a
great deal to have such friends as I have
got, and, Ray, what's the captainship after
all? I really don't envy the present captain
the least bit, though Forrest always seem to
think that I'm suffering and miserable about
it. I'll go on — and wait; and if the right
time ever comes, — well, there'll be time
enough to think about it then. And don't
keep your eyes open any longer for me, Ray,

but come to bed, for I'm getting warm as a toast."

Ray complied, and then the last lamp in the house was out, silence and peace settled down, and the long evening was ended

CHAPTER III.

PLOTTING.

GILBERT STARR soon recovered from
the effects of his plunge in the river,
though not in time to enjoy the skating, for
in a day or two the weather changed and
began to hint in earnest of spring. There
came days of warm rain and mist, and the
river began to peer through the ice in long
slender strips of dark water, and at last the
icy floor which had given the boys so much
delight, broke up, and went heaving and
tearing down to the sea.

And now that skating was really ended,
and there was no prospect of more winter
sports, Mr. Winterhalter's boys began to

think in earnest about examination, which was only a little way off. Some of the more studious had been preparing for it a great while, but the great mass of boys had been looking forward to the inevitable event with a certain dread and dislike, and now that the time was drawing near, took their books and settled down to hard study with many sighs and lamentations over the hardships of a schoolboy's life.

Of course they all expected that Gilbert Starr would keep the head-boy's place, and no one had any intention of trying for that position. Gilbert had filled it from the very first day that he became a member of the first class, and had held the place so long that no one thought of trying to oust him from it. In fact no one — even among his enemies, with the exception of Gates — wished for a change; and Gates wished for no change, unless he could slip into the position himself.

Now, as the days wore toward examination, Captain Philip began to think very deeply about the matter. It vexed him to think that, though Gilbert had lost the captaincy, he still outranked himself in virtue of being head-boy of the school; and though this high position did not give Gilbert much honor or pleasure, because all the boys had been turned against him, yet Gates longed for the place, and was vexed and irritated because there was no present prospect of getting it. "Why," he thought to himself, sitting by the window in the Boat Club's room one misty morning, "if I were head-boy and captain both, I should pretty much rule the school. Why, when I first came here, Gilbert Starr was looked up to as if he were a prince of the royal blood, and nobody thought of doing anything he objected to. But I spoiled that for him," Gates thought with a little malicious laugh, "and I don't think he'll ever get back to where he was before, not while I'm in the school, at any rate. But if he weren't head-boy—if I could only get the place—then he would be down entirely, and I should be at the top. I wish I knew how to do it!"

It was not an easy place to win, because it was only to be gained by hard study, and Gates was not particularly fond of such labor. And even if he was, there were Ray Hunter, Albert Turner and Barry White, who ranked above himself, and who would all have to be overcome. It seemed quite an impossibility, the whole of it, but Gates was loth to give up all hope, and sat long by the window trying to devise some plan by which he might obtain the position of head-boy.

Pretty soon Albert Turner came in, and he was just the person whom Gates wished to see. " Sit down," said he, " for I want to talk about the examination. Now who'll come out first in the struggle ? "

" Gilbert Starr, of course," said Turner; " I thought you knew that."

" Well, but is there no way by which some one else can get his position? "

" O yes, said Albert Turner, a little spitefully, " very easily. All one has got to do to get it is to study every night till twelve o'clock, review all that we've been over for the past year, besides getting the lessons that are given out every day ; then one will probably stand just about where Gilbert Starr stands, that is, if they are as smart; and all that's then necessary to secure the place is to know enough more than he does to come out best in the examination. I think it's very, very easy ; don't you? "

" Pshaw ! " said Captain Philip, angrily, " I'm in earnest about it, and I don't want to hear your nonsense."

"Nonsense or not," said Albert, "it's the truth."

"But Starr doesn't study like that," said Gates, "for he's always in bed when the rest of us are, and —"

"Well, of course he is," said Turner; "I was only telling you what one would have to do to catch up with him."

"And I don't believe he ever reviews," said the sceptical captain.

"There's where you don't know what you're talking about," said Albert; "Starr has got all the hard points and all the difficult solutions noted down — he did it as fast as he went along — and now all he has to do is to refer to his papers, instead of rummaging all his books over as the rest of us do. That's half the battle for him. I wish I'd done the same, but it's too late wishing, now."

Gates's face grew very bright. "How do

you know this is so, — about Starr's papers?" he asked.

"Because that used to be his way of doing when I was secretary of the club under him, and I had a chance to know; and I've heard Ray Hunter say the same thing within a week. But Starr does his work more thoroughly than he used to when he was Captain, because he has more time, I suppose."

A silence fell upon them, in which Turner picked up a book and began to study. At last Gates said, "I'd like to be head-boy very much."

"How strange!" said Turner, without looking off his book.

"But I don't see much hope of getting the place," continued Gates, "unless —"

"Unless what?" interrupted Turner, smiling at the idea that there was *any* probability of Captain Philip's success.

"Unless," said Gates slowly, and without looking at his companion, "I could get those papers of Gilbert Starr's."

Albert Turner's face grew very red quite suddenly, and as there was no apparent cause for any such change of countenance, you may as well know that Gates had unconsciously hit upon a plan which had been secretly harbored in Albert's own heart.

"I declare!" said Captain Philip, looking keenly into his companion's face, "I shouldn't wonder if you had thought of the same thing yourself."

"Stop!" said Turner, with a great show of indignation; "you've no right to talk to me like that! Do you know that if you were found out in such a thing you'd be disgraced and sent out of school?"

"Of course,—so do you. But I should look out for that matter. I'd go to work right, in the first place. I'd make friends of

all the Boat Club about the matter, and trust
to their honor. Then Gilbert Starr might
whistle for his papers, for who could prove
anything?"

"How do you know you could make
friends of us all?" said Turner, coldly.

"Pshaw!" said Gates, getting up and sitting down close to his companion, "don't
try to humbug me. I know well enough
that you'd all like to see Gilbert Starr
brought down."

"He's been brought down," said Turner,
trying to keep up an innocent appearance;
"why should I want him brought any
lower?"

"Nonsense!" said Captain Philip, "you're
only wasting breath. Do you suppose *I*
don't know *you*? and the rest of the fellows,
too? What did you pull Starr down for, if
it was not because you hated him? Tell me
that! And why have you all cut him?

And — but pshaw! it's only a waste of breath to talk about it. You'd all like to see Starr lose his position, and you can have the chance if you like. What do you say ? "

Now Albert Turner was not accustomed to this bold manner of talking about wicked and dishonorable plans, and he hardly knew what to say at first. But he was not an honorable boy, as you well remember from some events of the preceding summer, and as you will quickly perceive from the fact that he was not averse to listening to Gates's plan, and had even thought of it before the captain himself; and so he dallied with the temptation, pretending to hate it, yet encouraging the plan little by little, bringing all sorts of objections and scruples against it, while he was secretly intending to give aid to it, and at last, when Captain Philip had lost his patience and declared — " You're a confounded old hypocrite, Turner!" — he came out plumply, and said, "Yes, I agree to the plan."

"Of course you do," grumbled Gates, "and you might have said so without going such a long way round. I wonder if you think it's any better to sneak around for half an hour with your scruples, when you're all the time intending to give them up?"

Did you ever think which is worse: a boy who goes to work to do evil, making no pretence to goodness or honesty, or one who goes to work to compass the same evil end, and covers his intentions with a fair outside and a great pretence to virtue, while all the time the wickedness is working under the mask?

"Well," said Gates, after Albert Turner's decision had been made, "who shall do the difficult part of the plan? — taking the papers, I mean."

"You, of course," said Turner, getting up to go away.

But Gates pulled him back. "Wait," said he, "for I haven't got half through with you. If I have to do that part of the job, of course I'm to have the position to pay for it."

"Oh, ho!" said Albert, indignantly; "I'm to do all this to boost you into Gilbert's place, eh? and I may take a place under you after that, eh? Gates, did you ever hear of the monkey that used a cat's paws to get his chestnuts off the stove, and so kept his own from being burned?"

"I dare say I have," said Gates; "and what of it?"

"I'm not your cat, you see,—that's all."

"Very well," said Captain Philip, as if he were not at all displeased, "you may take the papers, and I'll stand down; that's fair, isn't it?"

Albert did not immediately reply. He had hardly sufficient courage to spy where Gilbert kept the coveted papers, and commit

a deliberate theft in taking them. He was
not as hardened as Gates, and the thought
of being the actual thief in the plot made
him shiver and tremble. He was suddenly
very sorry that he had conspired with the
captain. He looked up. "Gates," said he,
suddenly, and speaking sincerely this time at
least, "what a hard fellow you are!"

Captain Philip opened his eyes very wide
at this, saying, "What's that to do with your
decision?"

"Nothing, perhaps," Albert replied; "but
—but you may take the papers and have
the head-boy's place if you can.get it."

"Oh, don't be so polite," said Gates, laughing; "pray don't sacrifice all your plans on
my account!" But his companion turned
to the window without a word, and looked
out at the gray mist that lay over the land
and hid the river.

The first steps in a boy's downward

course are very easy to take, and he may not even know when he first turns his feet into the evil path. It had been so with Albert Turner. First, his straying from what was good and upright was so slight that he thought nothing of it, and it did not disturb him. He had gone down very slowly and gradually — erring in what seemed to him very little matters — till now it had come to this. He was not much given to reflection nor to regretting the past, but now, as he stood looking out upon the gloomy day, some very vivid remembrances of last summer's happy days came to him. What long and happy days they were! There was no Gates present with plots and troubling secrets; no discord nor enmity in the whole first class, and they were all very happy and contented with Gilbert for captain, and Gilbert to look up to and depend upon in all emergencies. He could not re-

member one day during the long winter that
had held so much genuine joy and content as
an hour of that past summer. Now, there
were wrangles, and everything and everybody were very disagreeable, he thought;
and altogether school was nothing at all the
pleasant place it used to be.

"However," he thought, "there's no use
in getting blue over it. I'm in the fix and
can't help myself." And with that he turned
around, saying, "Gates, if you're to have the
honor, to pay for your thieving, you'll have
to break the plan to the rest. I'm not going
to do it."

"Oh, trust me for that," said Gates, very
pleasantly. "I'll manage that nicely, and
just you see what a fluttering there is in the
nest, some of these mornings, when Starr
misses his papers!"

Albert Turner went down stairs very
much disgusted with the captain, the plot,

and himself in particular. But do *you* think that he was powerless to help himself out of the "fix," as he styled it? to tear himself away from Gates and his evil?

Now that Captain Philip had got the plan arranged to his mind, he went straightway at work to carry it out. He was cautious, at first, only dropping such hints now and then among his men as — "I say, Bob, wouldn't it be nice for me to beat Gil Starr out and out at the examination?" or, "What would you say, boys, if I got the head-boy's place for next term?"

Once, Tom Fowler answered this last question in his usual blunt way, by saying, "What would we say? why, we should most of us say that it was a dreadful misfortune for the school."

"Pshaw!" said the angry captain, "I won't bear your nonsense. But do you know I'm in earnest about it?"

In this manner, and by keeping the subject continually before the boys, Gates brought them to understand, without having said so much in words, that they need not be surprised to see Gilbert Starr lose his rank in some mysterious manner at the coming examination.

"If there's any trick about it — and you may be sure there is if Gates has anything to do with it — I say it's a confounded shame!" said Tom; "however, it's none of my bread and butter. We all cut loose from Gilbert long ago, and I suppose it won't do to tattle."

Boys are not usually very vehement for the right; and the boys of the Boat Club were like all others. If one of their number had had the courage and zeal to make a stand against their captain's machinations, they would all have followed this one, and Gates and his evil would have been overthrown. But as it was, no one stirred about the matter, assuring themselves that it was no affair of theirs, and Captain Philip met no opposition and found no obstacle in his way. So it came about that one night, after all the rest were asleep, the plotting captain removed Gilbert's precious packet from the little table by his bedside, and took it to a hiding place of his own. And only Albert Turner knew where it was concealed, Gates being quite too wise to entrust the secret to more than one beside himself.

CHAPTER IV.

GILBERT'S DISMAY.

PHILIP GATES removed Gilbert's packet of papers on Saturday night. As the next day was Sunday, of course they were not missed; and it was not until Monday morning, about an hour before recitations, that Gilbert ran up to his room after them. He was in a great hurry, having been detained past his usual study-hour, and was was much astonished — not to say vexed — to find his packet gone. "Where could I have put it?" he said, standing by the little table at the head of his bed and gazing wonderingly at the place where he was sure it had lain on the previous Saturday night.

61

Then he searched in the little drawer underneath the table, but there was nothing there but two or three torn leaves of school-books and some old letters of Ray's. "Well, this *is* curious!" he thought to himself; "I wonder if I'm getting so absent-minded that I don't know where I leave my papers?"

He opened his trunk and searched among the clothing there, simply because he could not think of any other place to search, and knowing well enough that it was not there. He closed the lid with a very puzzled face. There was no other hiding-place for the packet amongst his things, and consequently no where else to look. Remembering that it was already past time for him to be at work upon his lessons, he grew more and more impatient. Ray's papers and his own were all together, and suddenly thinking that there was a possibility that his packet might be hidden among them, Gilbert hastily got up and looked them all over one by one, but with no better success. Then he discovered that Gates was sitting in a far corner of the room, very busily studying his lesson; but failed to see that whenever his own face was turned in another direction Gates's was very busily studying *him*.

Gilbert sat down and thought about the matter for five minutes. But the mystery was as great as ever at the end of that time, and gave no sign of ever becoming clearer. He got up and went to the table that stood between the next row of beds, and although it did not belong to him, took the liberty to look upon it. It was a right which the boys never disputed, and Gilbert's own table was very often searched by some member of the class. But Gates left his corner and came down to where Gilbert stood, very savage and very important.

"Look here," said he, for once deigning

to speak to Gilbert, "what right have you
to be meddling with other people's tables?"

Gilbert took no more notice of him than
if he had not spoken, and this inattention,
you must know, was very aggravating to
a fellow of such importance as Gates. He
grew very red and angry.

"Do you know," said he, laying a heavy
hand on Gilbert's arm, "that I am captain
of the Boat Club, and won't allow my men
to be imposed upon by such as *you*?"

Valiant Captain Philip intended that this
"*you*" should be very scornful and very
insulting. Therefore it was not pleasant for
him to have Gilbert shake his hand lightly
off, and, while a faint smile curled up the
corner of his mouth, proceed with his search
as if he were entirely unaware that Gates
was near. Then, finding that his packet
was not there, Gilbert went back to his own
table. But Gates's pride was too thoroughly

wounded to allow him to give up the matter thus, and so he followed Gilbert, and thus did a very unwise thing.

"Oh, you may please to be silent about it," said he, sneeringly, " but that won't do. I demand to know what you were overhauling my men's tables for! What right had you there?"

Gilbert took up a book and said nothing, though his hands twitched as if they longed to get Gates by the shoulders, and were only held back by a very strong effort. Very likely Gates did not know Gilbert as the rest did, having seen less of him during his short stay in the school than almost any other boy, or he never would have gone to the length he did. Failing to make any impression by demands and threats, he taunted Gilbert with being a hypocrite; adding — "If I couldn't do better than you've done by turning traitor to my company, and getting made

over into such a milk-and-water affair as you
are, I'd sell out my stock in trade and go
into the milliner's bus — "

Suddenly, without having the remotest
idea how it happened, Gates found himself
in a very awkward position indeed. His
feet were on the floor, but his body was bent
over the foot of one of the beds in an
exceedingly uncomfortable manner, and Gilbert's gray eyes were looking down upon
him, full of fire and disgust.

"You've given your opinion of me, free
gratis," said he, holding Gates down, while
his words came very slowly, he was so
angry, "and now you shall have my opinion
of yourself. I think if I had such a small,
mean, contemptible nature as you've got,
I'd — I'd — really, I can't think of any occu-
pation that would be small enough for you.
You could'nt grasp the mysteries of the
milliner's trade, and —— Oh, but I've good

mind to strike you!" said Gilbert, abruptly, remembering, while the hot, passionate blood reddened his face, certain insulting epithets which Gates had applied to him in times past. Somebody came running up stairs, three steps at a bound, and came along the hall, whistling and singing by turns, and pushed open the door.

It was Ray Hunter, and he stopped short in the doorway, exclaiming, after a second's pause, " Good heavens! Gilbert, what are you about?"

" I'm considering whether I'd better give this fellow a thrashing or not," said Gilbert, hotly, and without looking around; "what do you advise?"

Ray made no reply at first. He would doubtless have rejoiced to see Gates thrashed, and would have liked to lent a hand, as for that matter; but there was something else to be thought of.

Did you ever think what a great and important thing it is to be the friend of another? to be loved, trusted, confided in and leaned upon? Ray had never thought greatly of it before, but now it flashed upon him like a new revelation. Here was Gilbert, who had lost his temper and was unable to judge as he ought; and he had asked his advice. What should he tell him? Every desire and inclination of his heart bade him say, " Yes! thrash Gates!"—but this new sense of the importance of the decision made him remember it was for Gilbert's good, and not for his own gratification, that he was to advise. For once, at least, I think Ray was a model friend, for putting away all thoughts of his own gratifition, and looking only for Gilbert's good, he came up to the opponents, and, laying his hand on Gilbert's shoulder, said — " Gil, old fellow, I'd like you to thrash him very much, but you see, I don't think it would be quite square with what you are trying to do for yourself — making yourself a better fellow, you know — and for that reason, though of course it makes no odds with me, I — I — well, I wouldn't thrash him, Gilbert."

Gates was freed in an instant, and Gilbert turned around to Ray, grasping both his hands and saying, vehemently, " O, Ray Hunter, what a friend you are to me ! "

" There," said this friend of Gilbert's, pretending not to be affected by Gilbert's gratefulness, " don't say any more about such a little matter. I'll be in the same fix, likely enough, some time."

Gilbert's face grew very sober when he turned back and looked at Gates, whose face was very crimson with mortified pride and smothered anger, and who was very busily dusting his jacket; and looking at him, Gilbert had a struggle with himself. Whatever

the feeling was against which he was con-
tending, he managed to conquer it at last,
and went up to his enemy, holding out his
hand.

"Gates," said he, frankly, "I was very
quick just now. I don't suppose we shall be
very good friends, but I'd like to shake
hands with you over it."

Captain Philip withdrew his hand and
frowned heavily. "I'll not shake hands!"
he muttered; "this is not to be the end of
the matter."

"Why not?" said Gilbert, pleasantly, and
still extending his hand.

"No; keep your hand to yourself!" said
Gates, "for I'm not going to touch it."

Then Gilbert withdrew his hand, and the
captain picked his book from off the floor
where it had fallen in the encounter, and
went out without another word.

"Now," said Ray, as the door closed, "how

"I should like to shake hands with you over it." Page 70.

on earth came you and Gates to get into a squabble? I thought he wouldn't speak to you."

This question brought back to Gilbert the remembrance of his loss, which, in his trouble with Gates, he had entirely forgotten. And so without answering Ray's question, he asked one himself.

"Oh," said he, "but · have you seen any thing of my papers? — the little packet that held all the reviews which we are to go over."

"No," said Ray, "but it's on our table, of course; and what has that to do with fighting Gates?"

"But it's not on our table," said Gilbert, "and I'm afraid it's gone entirely."

"But you left it there?"

"Yes."

"Then some one has helped himself to it," said Ray; "but, if you please, I'd like to know how you got into trouble with Gates."

"Oh," said Gilbert, "I was hunting for my papers and took the liberty to look on that table out yonder,—Tom Fowler's, you know, —and Gates came down to interfere. But I didn't mind him at all, and I suppose that made him mad, for he followed me out here to my own table and got very insulting. And then I—got mad. I'm very sorry for it. Gates isn't worth minding, and I oughtn't to have minded him. I'm glad I didn't thrash him, but I believe I should have done so if you hadn't put the right thought into my head just at that moment. Do you remember that proverb in Bob Upham's old book—'A faithful friend is a strong defence?'—Well, I believe it's true of my friend, anyhow!" and Gilbert took Ray's hand and pressed it gratefully.

All this made Ray very happy, but, like most boys, he was averse to showing the emotion, and so said, hastily, "But your papers! the loss of those is more than all the rest. But they must be around somewhere; I can't believe any of the fellows would be mean enough to take them!"

To satisfy himself, he got up and made a thorough search of the table, the drawer, as well as a hasty inspection of the other tables in the room. He came back to Gilbert, looking very blank.

"You're right," said he; "the packet is gone."

"And gone at a most unfortunate time, too," said Gilbert; "it's only a little over a week and a half, you know, to examination day."

"Sure enough!" said Ray, with a start; "and I'm not sure but that is the reason why it is gone. Just think, Gilbert! if one were mean enough, one might take your papers and prevent you from keeping your head-boy's place!"

"I have thought of that," said Gilbert, soberly.

But it was a new thought for Ray, and kept him silent for nearly five minutes. At the end of that time he jumped up and exclaimed, "The more I think of it, the surer I am that some one has been thieving! Of course your papers didn't take wings—there were so many monstrous heavy problems in them, that they couldn't fly if they tried— and seriously, it looks like a plot to get you out of the head-boy's place; and if it *is* a plot, there isn't but one fellow in school that's mean enough or wicked enough to serve you so, and that's the one who just went out this door; and Gil, I wish you'd given him a good thrashing while it was so convenient!"

"Well," said Gilbert, after a long silence, "will you grant me a favor?"

"Yes; it's granted already."

"Then please not to say a word about my loss till I give you permission."

Ray's face fell. "Now!" he exclaimed, "is that fair?"

"I think so. You see, there is not the slightest suspicion to put upon any one, and what would be the use of telling every one of my loss? But if we are silent about it something may occur that will lead us the right way."

Ray acquiesced.

A week passed, however, without anything having occurred. The mystery remained the same, and there was no clue by which to unravel it, nor was there any definite suspicion to attach to any member of the class. Gilbert was somewhat dismayed at the prospect before him, — examination day only half-a-week off, and no apparent hope that he should ever see his much-needed papers again, — but still resolutely kept his loss to himself, and waited.

Ray was much more anxious and indignant than his friend, and stormed and threatened the whole class with vengeance whenever Gilbert and he were alone. He came to his friend one night, begging to be released from the promise which he had given.

"I was rash that time!" he said, laughing; "but were you quite fair? Now release me, and you'll never be sorry!"

"What are you going to do if I release you?" Gilbert asked.

Ray hesitated a while, but finally said, "Well, I'm going to carry the whole matter before Mr. Winterhalter. He's got power, and he can make the thief give up the plunder, or at least discover him. If I don't do so, you'll just say nothing and lose your rank without a word, and no one will ever know that you've been wronged. I won't have it so!" said Ray, with energy, "and I want Gates, — for I know he's the thief, — brought to justice. Do you know? — the sneaking fellow has told all the fellows that you knocked him down when his back was turned toward you, and. that you did it out of spite and envy because he has your old rank. Of course I denied it! and I told him to his face that he was a sneak, and I don't know but we should have had a fight right there in the hall, if Mr. Winterhalter hadn't happened to come in."

But Gilbert held Ray to his promise, much to that young gentleman's indignation.

" I wouldn't like," Gilbert said, "to have the whole school turned into an uproar because my papers are missing. It would be a long and tedious job, and even if it was successful, it's too late to do any good."

This was no consolation to Ray, however.

CHAPTER V.

A S the third day before examination came, Ray Hunter resolved that he would reveal Gilbert's loss to Mr. Winterhalter, whether Gilbert gave him permission or not. " It's for Gilbert's good," he thought, " and what a shame 'twill be to have him fail before all the people at examination, and to have everybody think that it was because he didn't study and work hard enough. Oh, that rascally Gates! I told Gilbert how t'would be the first day that Gates came here. I knew that they couldn't both rule, and Gates don't care how low he stoops if only he *can* rule ; but Gilbert can't be mean if he

78

tries, and so Captain Philip has the advantage of him; but I'd like to expose the rascal! I'd just like Mr. Winterhalter and everybody to find out about him!"

But Ray had a lingering fear that Gilbert would be very much displeased if the promise which he had given was not faithfully kept, and so all the third day before the coming event he was very anxious and undecided, and thought so much about the matter that his lessons suffered considerably. He came to a decision at last, by saying, " I'll wait till to-morrow morning, and if nothing happens before that time, I'll go to Mr. Winterhalter, *anyhow*. It's for Gilbert's good, and I can afford to bear his displeasure a while."

Now this evening of the third day proved to be a rainy one. It was not a blustering night, but the rain poured steadily, without any lull or slacking, and the eaves kept up

their heavy drip, drip, and the drops dashed
against the panes, and altogether it was just
such a night as one loves to spend before
the fire, listening to the down-pour without.
So, though every one ought to have been
busy with his books in preparation for what
the next day but one was to bring, Mr.
Winterhalter's boys were gathered in the
school-room, chatting, telling stories, and
making as merry as they might. The lamp-
light was not so bright but that the room
was pleasantly dim, and they had gathered
together as inclination prompted, — here a
little group withdrawn to hear some wonderful tale, and there a boisterous crowd of
twenty or thirty who welcomed every addi-
tion to their number, and seemed to think
they could not be too numerous or too
noisy.

But Gilbert Starr, having been "cut" by
his companions, sat all alone by one of the

windows where the rain dashed loudest. Ray had vanished somewhere in the noisy crowd, and Perry Kent had hidden himself away to have a quiet hour with his lessons.

Very likely some sad and sorrowful thoughts crept into Gilbert's heart as he sat here, quite deserted, and looked around him at the merry and happy groups. Once, he remembered, there was not one of those present who would have thought their circle complete without him; nor one who would not have thought it a great honor to sit beside him.

Now, how changed it all was! No one cared for his company, or, at least, they pretended they did not, and he might have been a bench or a chair for all the attention they paid him. And all this neglect was because he chose to do what he thought was right,—what he *knew* was right. "It's very strange that just doing right should have

brought all this about," Gilbert thought;
"and it *does* seem as if there never was to
be an end to it!" Then he had been robbed
of his papers, and his rank was in all probability to be lost to him after two short days,
and altogether he felt very much disgusted
and down-hearted at the moment. "I declare!" he thought, bitterly, "if it weren't for
Ray and Perry and the Winterhalters, I believe I'd pack my trunk and leave school
to-morrow morning."

Now, as you know well enough, this was
not Gilbert Starr in his own naturally cheerful and courageous spirit. The loss of his
papers, and the prospect of the loss of his
rank, had disheartened him; and the patter
of the rain that to the merry crowd was
cheerful, to him sounded only sad and cheerless. He did not remove himself from the
sound of its wailing, however, but sat listening to it with a dull aching in his heart,

thinking, as he looked out in the black depths of the night, that there was not a more solitary fellow in the wide earth than himself; which thought was quite untrue, as he himself would have remembered at any other time.

It was not long, however, before Perry Kent made his appearance. "Why, Gilbert," said he, smiling, " you look very lonesome ! "

Gilbert would not confess to any such weakness, however, but said, " I'm sick of this school ! In fact, I hate it ; and I've half a good mind to leave it forever to-morrow morning." Perry's shocked face made his protector laugh, in spite of his gloominess. " Come," said Gilbert, " don't look like that long at a time, or I shall lose all my misery at once. I can't stand such a startled countenance ! "

" But," said the boy, " you wouldn't go away and leave Ray and Mr. and Mrs. Winterhalter, and — and me, Gilbert ? "

"Well, I don't know but I should be obliged to," said Gilbert, gravely; "I couldn't carry you *all* in my trunk, for Mr. Winterhalter is decidedly a big man, and might object to such close quarters as I should have to give him; and Ray is quite a tall fellow, and I can't think of any way by which he might be folded up, and you — well, you *are* small and I guess I could tuck you in somewhere."

Perry laughed, and drew a long breath of relief.

"You were joking!" he said, "and. I'm glad of it, for, if you left school, how could I stay here? and oh, just think of it, Gilbert! you're to graduate next fall, and I've got to stay till — till I'm a great grown boy, at least. But there's another reason why you oughtn't to leave school, — why you never will, I'm sure.

"Well, what's that?" said Gilbert, pleasantly.

"Because, if you ran away from your
trouble, and so gave up to it —"

"I should be a coward and all that, I
suppose." interrupted Gilbert; "well, you
needn't be alarmed, — I'll put off going to-
morrow morning, I guess."

And here Ray joined them, very merry
and cheerful from the company he had just
quitted, and the first thing he said to Gilbert,
was, "Well, you've improved wonderfully in
the last ten minutes. Only that length of
time ago I looked out this way, and your
face was about twice the length of my arm,
and not quite half as broad. When I saw it,
I thought, 'Well, you'd better get over that
way, Ray Hunter, before Gilbert gets desperate and dashes his brains out.' So I've
come ; but Perry's ahead of me, as usual."

"The first thing he said to me," said
Perry, "was that he thought of leaving
school to-morrow morning."

"Leaving school?" cried Ray; "that's a pretty story! I'd like to see him undertake it. What on earth would he leave school for?" But without waiting for any one to answer his question, Ray hastily added, "Come up stairs, Gilbert. 'Tisn't pleasant for you down here; but up there we can be quiet and cosey. Come along without a word, as I tell you. And you come too, Perry!" for Ray's prejudice toward the boy had entirely vanished since Gilbert's mishap on the ice.

The three made their way between the groups out of the room, and went up stairs. And there they spent a very pleasant evening, and Gilbert declared that he felt wonderfully lighter-hearted, and was quite sure that for once he had had a touch of the blues, — "just enough, you know," he said to Ray, "to make everything look gloomy."

Perry Kent got sleepy and went to bed,

and Ray and Gilbert prepared to follow, though it was not quite nine and the boys had not left the school-room. Ray was the first to get into bed, but stepped out again very suddenly.

"What's the trouble?" queried Gilbert, laughing a little.

"Look here!" cried Ray; "I'd just like to know what you call this, old fellow?" and plunging his hand down between the sheets, he drew out Gilbert's precious and long-lost packet of papers.

There was a dead silence, in which the friends stared at each other in utter bewilderment. Then Gilbert said, "Did you mean that for a surprise to me?" and Ray cried, "Did you mean that for a surprise for me?" And then they both exclaimed, "No!" with one breath.

"Then where did it come from, and are you sure it's mine?" said Gilbert, doubting his own eyes.

"Of course I am! I should know your handwriting if you wrote Chinese; and here are all your problems plain as day, and the whole packet as neat as a pin. Whoever has had it knew enough to be choice of it. And here is — Ah, here is a note!" said Ray, suddenly, as a bit of paper fluttered out to the floor.

Gilbert picked it up, and found only these words within:

"G. S.

There's a plot against you; but here are your papers from one who has repented his part in the affair. Don't betray me."

And that was all. The writer had signed no name, and evidently intended to keep his identity a secret. Gilbert handed the note to Ray with a very blank face, and took up his mysteriously-returned papers.

"There! didn't I tell you so?" said Ray,

as he finished the note ; " didn't I tell you
there was a plot against you in the first
place ? But there's more than one concerned in it, and I thought it was only
Gates. And who could have repented at
this late day ? "

" It's all a mystery," said Gilbert, busy
with his papers; " but I'm rejoiced to see
them again, you may believe."

" Of course ! " said Ray, suddenly very
glad that he had put off telling Mr. Winter-
ter; " but oh, why couldn't he have repented
a week ago? — and how on earth does he
suppose you're going to betray him as long
as you haven't the slightest idea who he
is ? "

" He means, I suppose, that I'm not to
betray to any one that my papers are returned to me."

" Then you'll have to be spry," said Ray,
hastily getting into bed, " for there goes the
bell, and there come the fellows, pell-mell."

Gilbert followed just as the door opened to admit Gates and the rest of the class, and ensured the safety of his packet by putting it under his pillow. It did not take long for the room to settle down to quietness, and then Ray began to whisper so many conjectures concerning the mysterious affair, that it was fully an hour before they were both asleep. Gilbert fancied himself to be pretty certain that this unknown friend was Tom Fowler. He thought the awkward handwriting resembled that young gentleman's very much; but as Ray did not seem to suspect any such thing, he was silent about his own suspicions, and went to sleep very grateful toward some unknown friend in his class. But when he awoke the next morning, the event of the previous evening seemed so much like a dream, that he had to put his hand under the pillow to assure himself that it was all a reality.

He was standing at the foot of the stairs

when the members of his class came down
to breakfast, and there was not a face that he
did not scan long and attentively; but his
scrutiny was all without result. He fancied
Al Turner colored a little under his gaze, but
thought little about it, — partly because he
thought Al would be the last person to
repent of such a deed if once committed,
and partly because he could not convince
himself that his old secretary would stoop to
such a meanness and wickedness as downright theft. And so he made up his mind
that it was Tom Fowler to whom he was
indebted, — thus hitting very wide of the
mark.

As soon as breakfast was over, Gilbert
hurried back up-stairs to his precious packet.
" Oh, if I had but had it a week ago ! " he
thought, with a bitter feeling welling up in
his heart towards Gates. He had meant to
pass the examination very skilfully, if not

even brilliantly, and the thought of so doing
had done a great deal toward consoling him
for being shut out from the society of his
old comrades; but here was all hope of a
brilliant, or even tolerable examination, cut
off by the maliciousness of — who? Gates,
he was sure; and the thought made his
breath come thick and fast, and the hot blood
swell in his veins. He felt, just then, as if
it would be a great satisfaction to have
Gates in the same position in which he had
had him once before, and to have no one
interfere. But then, what good would it do,
after all?

Gilbert sat down to his papers with a
sigh, and prepared to settle down to hard
work; but before he had read a line, Ray
came scampering up-stairs in his usual headlong manner, and burst in upon his friend
with a great clatter.

"Oh, you needn't look so disappointed,"

said he, instantly changing his bustling manner; "I've come to help you. Show me where you begin, and I'll look out the answers to your problems, while you copy them."

"But your own lessons?"

"Are all right! don't you mind."

"But, Ray —"

"Pshaw! I won't take a word from you;" and he sat down resolutely beside Gilbert and went to work. They worked steadily till it was time for recitations,— Ray, very patient and careful.

When evening came, Gilbert withdrew to a silent corner of the school-room, where he was soon absorbed in his books and papers, and was not disturbed till he felt a hand laid upon his shoulder. It was Ray again, pencil and paper in hand.

"Now look here," protested Gilbert, "go to your own books. I'll manage, somehow."

"I won't," said Ray, stoutly, and sat down.

"But you aren't fair to yourself," said Gilbert; "you might win my place if you'd only study and make an effort."

"There, don't be foolish, Gilbert, dear," said Ray. "Just as if we weren't friends?"

Was it not something to be such friends as they were?

CHAPTER VI.

GATES'S DISMAY.

THE remaining day before examination wore around with hard study on the part of many besides Gilbert Starr, though may be he sat longest into the night and worked hardest, and the morning of the important day dawned very sunny and spring-like. All the boys in Gilbert's room were up early, some to snatch a few last minutes at their books, and some to spend the time in the preparation of unusually nice toilets, — a practice, you know, which boys are not greatly addicted to, except on such important occasions as examination-day.

Captain Philip Gates was very smiling and agreeable to every one, and did not disdain to notice Gilbert with a condescending nod, which Ray had the bad manners to laugh at. And breakfast came very early, in order that every one might have time to prepare for the opening exercises, which were to begin at ten; and after breakfast they returned to books or toilets, just as they were minded.

Gilbert finished his own dressing for the occasion in a very few minutes, and went back to his books; but Ray lingered before the glass that hung over their table, and lingered so long that Gilbert at last looked up from his papers, smiling a little.

"Well," said Ray, laughing, "you may smile if you like, but I never saw my hair, collar, or necktie, act half so bad at any other time when I didn't care particularly about 'em. Of course, all three of them know that it's examination-day, and are on a

strife to do their worst. But go on with
your books, Gil,— I'll get through in the
course of the day."

Gilbert went on with his studying, but
Ray presently exclaimed, — " There was one
thing I was going to keep for a surprise for
you, old fellow, but I expect that it's all up
now. Mother was to come on and so be
here at examination, and I was the happiest
fellow all last week, thinking about it; but
that letter I had last night said that her
coming was all uncertain, because father's
business kept him back, and she'd have to
come alone if she came at all. But I shall
look for her, yet ; and I want you to see her,
old fellow ! She's the best mother a fellow
ever had, and I meant to surprise you by
taking you down into Mrs. Winterhalter's
parlor and introducing you all of a sudden. I
declare," Ray added, as an after-thought,
" if I were to graduate at college and take

all the honors, I don't believe father 'd think
he could leave his business long enough to
see me do it. But mother — well, just wait
till you see her, Gilbert."

Which Gilbert said he would endeavor to
do, and went on with his studies. But Ray
was too light of heart to keep silent long at
a time, and presently exclaimed — " Look
here, Gilbert, you're the funniest fellow !
You didn't spend ten minutes getting ready,
when you're head-boy, and everybody, of
course, will look at you before the rest."

" They 'll not want to look long," said
Gilbert, " after they hear what a miserable
review I've got to offer them. Oh, Ray, but
I'm tempted, you don't know *how* hard, to
lay hands on Gates every time I meet him."

" I wish it was best ! " said Ray, quickly ;
" but it wouldn't quite do, and I'm awful
sorry about it. But wait," he suddenly
added, " there's one way we *can* do. I

haven't the scruples you have, you know, and I'll thrash him for you. I'm not quite his height, but I can do it; what do you say, Gilbert?"

Gilbert smiled at the novel method of giving Gates his deserts. "Thank you," said he; " but let's drop the subject. I'm in a furious hurry, and it don't help me any to talk about Gates."

" That's a hint for me to keep quiet," said Ray, " and I'll take it." And hardly had he spoken this, when the door opened, and in trooped Gates and his men after their books and papers.

Captain Philip regarded Gilbert rather keenly as he sat poring over his books, and mentally wondered if he had any thought of success. Gates desired very much to discern some trace of anxiety or depression upon Gilbert's countenance; but finding none, consoled himself with thinking, " He wouldn't show it if he was certain that he was going to fail,— he's got such a will of his own. But I wonder how he'll look when I come to step into the head-boy's place and he has to step out?"

This thought was so pleasant to the valiant captain. that it comforted him for Gilbert's present unconcern, and presently he went off, with all his men, in the gayest of spirits.

Ray said, "Do you see how confident Gates is? Now, I'm ready to go down, too; when will you come?"

Gilbert looked at his watch, and said, "It's only half-past nine, and as I can't spare a minute, I shan't be down till Mr. Winterhalter rings for us." After which Ray departed, and Gilbert was alone. He thought he had never known a half-hour so short. He had placed his watch on the table by his side, and was almost dismayed to see how fearfully fast the little golden hands traveled over the half-circle. There was such a vast quantity of things that he must leave unreviewed! — so much that he could not but fail in! — and when he thought of what a perfect, and perhaps brilliant examination he might have passed but for the wrong that had been done him — Well, do you greatly wonder that his hands felt very much like doubling themselves up into fists, and that his breath came hot and quick?"

The half-hour came to an end, and Mr. Winterhalter's bell rang, — the signal for gathering together in the hall. Gilbert closed his book, picked up his papers, and after hurriedly brushing his hair, went down. Ray met him at the foot of the stairs.

"There's a great crowd of people in the school-room, and it's packed full, except, of course, where we are to sit. And you'll have to hurry a bit, too!"

Now it was Gilbert's duty, as head-boy, to arrange the classes in their order and to marshal them into the audience-room to their seats. Mr. Winterhalter had nothing at all to do with this, and had already taken his chair with the grave-looking men who had come to aid in the examination. Of course, Gates had to submit to his rival, and be placed as he chose to place him, but the captain consoled himself with thinking that it was the last time that Gilbert Starr would ever give orders to *him*. Then they filed up the long aisle, between the crowd, to their seats in front, and during the ten minutes that elapsed while Gilbert was getting all the classes seated, Gates was very self-satisfied and exultant, thinking that at the next examination he should receive all the admiration that his rival was now receiving.

"It *is* an honor to be head-boy," he thought, as he watched Gilbert walking up and down the aisle beside the classes that were filing into their seats; "and Starr looks very handsome doing the thing, but next term!—ah, where will he be then?"

If the captain had taken more thought for his own whereabouts at that far-distant day, he would have done much better than to have troubled himself about Gilbert's welfare.

Then, the school being all seated, the examination shortly commenced. It began with the under classes, with whom you are unacquainted, and so will not care to hear about; though these smaller boys had by far the greater number of parents and friends among the audience. The Second Class came next, and Perry Kent was very successful, as Gilbert was sure he would be; and not until half-past eleven were the boys of the First Class called. Mr. Winterhalter looked at them with a little thrill of pride.

"Ah," said he, in a whisper to one of the spectacled doctors, "they're a noble set of fellows. You may ply my head-boy, there, with as hard questions as you like, for he's equal to it. I haven't the least fear for him, and the harder you work at him the better."

Poor Mr. Winterhalter! you were doomed to disappointment that time.

The examination of the First Class did not open very brilliantly. Gilbert did not appear very enthusiastic, and simply made very brief answers to the questions asked him.

"Is he ill, or what?" wondered the principal. The doctors went on with their wise questioning, and Mr. Winterhalter began to grow nervous. He wondered what made Gilbert so dull and common-place in his replies, and looked at him with a troubled face which Gilbert did not fail to note. Then old Doctor Wayne, who was a college

professor, spoke up and propounded a difficult problem in mathematics. There was a
short space of silence and reflection on the
part of the class, then Gilbert raised his
hand in token of having solved it. Mr. Winterhalter's face brightened.

"Ah, he'll come to it, pretty quick," he
thought. But just then Gates raised his
hand to show that he had solved it, too. Mr.
Winterhalter was very much surprised at
this unusual smartness on the part of the
captain, and still more so when Gates's answer proved to be correct, and the same as
Gilbert's. He did not notice how his head-
boy bit his lips, nor the two bright spots
of anger that suddenly came into his cheeks
and as suddenly faded. Then, as it was
noon, the examination was put over till after
dinner, the crowd dispersed till it was time
for the exercises to re-open, and the boys
went off to their noon meal in the dining-

room, and the doctors to their repast, which was served in Mr. Winterhalter's parlor. Ray found Gilbert as soon as possible.

" Don't you mind! " said he, comfortingly; " you're even with Gates, and that's some consolation."

But Gilbert *did* mind. " I might as well give it up," he said, bitterly; — " Gates has copied all my answers, — that's plain enough! "

" Yes; but you'll make that all up when you get out of mathematics. Just wait, — don't give it up! Oh, but if you let Gates beat you, I shall want to go and hide myself."

Gilbert said not another word, but ate his dinner and took a hurried look into his books. The crowd took their seats again, the bell rang, the old doctors gathered on the platform, and Mr. Winterhalter saw the classes file in again with a more hopeful heart.

"Gilbert has been reserving himself for the afternoon," he thought, "and I shall have no reason to be disappointed in him." Yet he had a secret dread that again his head-boy would prove dull. The exercises opened with some questions from old Doctor Wayne that proved too much for all but Gilbert, and he answered them with his old ease and readiness. Mr. Winterhalter was delighted, and said to himself, "It's just as I thought; he was waiting for afternoon."

Then the old doctor took up one of the lesson-books and began to review. The whole class did well till it came to solving problems, and then there was a sudden falling off in the answers. The rivalry went back to Gates and Gilbert again, and the the audience decided that the honor of head-boy's position would rest upon one of them. Mr. Winterhalter could hardly contain his surprise at Gates's quickness and -

correctness. He began to think that the captain had been a very smart scholar in disguise. He looked at the papers which he held, and found that Gates had correctly answered as many questions as Gilbert himself.

"Really," thought he, " this is very astonishing. Gilbert will have to look out for his position."

Now Gates was quite as much astonished at Gilbert's quickness and correctness. He had expected that his rival would utterly fail as soon as the exercises were well under way ; but here was Gilbert answering question after question, and correctly solving problem after problem. What could it mean ? As soon as Gates had fairly got Gilbert's papers into his possession, his first care was to copy them, and then to hide the original packet away that it might not be seen in his hands; and from that time

until the present, he had not looked at it.
The idea that it could by any possibility get
back to Gilbert's hands, had never entered
his head, and now that his rival showed
such wonderful correctness, he began to be
very much alarmed and dismayed.

Doctor Wayne, the old professor of mathematics, laid down his book at last, with one
last problem. It was very difficult, but
Gates recognized it instantly. He had
found it written out very carefully in Gilbert's packet, and at once held up his hand,
thinking, " Now, Gilbert Starr, I've got you !
you can't answer that." But after a moment's reflection, Gilbert's hand came up,
too, and Gates was so dismayed at the sight
that he stammered, got confused and gave in
the wrong answer after all, while Gilbert
gave in the right one. Captain Philip mentally gave up the struggle then ; and the
old doctor dismissed them with a good many

compliments. A short intermission followed. Gilbert and Gates took their seats amid
a little murmur of applause,— Gilbert very
grave and rather stern, and Gates very
smiling, though secretly he was very un-
easy. He began to suspect that Gilbert had
regained his packet in some mysterious
manner, and if he *had* regained it, of course
he must know that he had been dealt foully
by. And what would be the consequences?
Gates's stolen plumes began to trouble him
very much. He began to feel that there
was danger and disgrace ahead of him.

In the short intermission, Ray had time to
shake Gilbert's hand and whisper, "The rascal came near beating you, but he's done
his worst! You'll have it all your own
way now, and so do your best, and bring
down the house just as you always do!"

And Perry Kent passed a little note
across the boys' shoulders, which said,

" DEAR GILBERT,

Don't get discouraged! I was dreadfully afraid that wicked Gates was going to beat you, but ho can't do you any more hurt. Now be just as smart as you can, and make up for all that's happened.

PERRY."

Gilbert smiled at this message of his protege's, and looked back to him and nodded assuringly. And both Ray and Perry took heart when they saw how calmly and confidently ho went back with his class at Mr. Winterhalter's call. Gates knew that it was now no use to strive for his rival's position, and suddenly grew very dull. Albert Turner, Barry White, and even Bob Upham, showed to much better advantage than ho. Their scholarship, even in mathematics, was much higher, in reality, than his ; but they had not had the advantage of Gilbert's solutions. Now that Gates was obliged to fall back upon his own attainments, his brilliancy and correctness were all gone. And, as Ray said, Gilbert had it all his own way. His answers were quick and prompt, and delighted Mr. Winterhalter very much. He listened and rubbed his hands softly together in the exuberance of his delight, and at last leaned over and whispered in old Doctor Wayne's ear, "What did I tell you? Solid, sir,— solid to the very foundation! I hope Bainsley will keep him translating by the hour together, if he likes. I'll warrant that he can't puzzle him."

"He's very fair, very fair," said the old doctor, likewise rubbing his hands; "send him to our college when you get through with him."

It came to an end at last, and Professor Bainsley, who was much younger than the other wise men, stepped out and shook Gilbert's hand, saying before the whole company, "I am very glad to know you, sir!"

Then the murmur of applause ran up and down the room, and in very deep silence Mr. Winterhalter stepped out and formerly re-instated Gilbert in his position of head-boy, then allowed him to go down to his class, while up and down ran the clamor of applause again. Then, after a few prizes had been distributed to the under classes, the exercises were over, and the long-looked for day was ended. The crowd was a long time in dispersing, for there were fathers and mothers looking for their boys, and boys looking for their parents, and there were a great many going home to spend vacation.

The doctors and professors came down from their platform, and found it but a slow process getting to Mr. Winterhalter's parlor. Gilbert had kept his seat, waiting for the crowd to thin, and was quite alone, for Ray had suddenly darted away from his side into the crowd, and had not yet returned. Sud-

denly a hand was laid upon his shoulder,
and looking up, there stood Professor Bainsley, who had got thus far on his way to the
parlor.

"I congratulate you," he said, smiling,
and shaking Gilbert's hand; "when do you
graduate?"

"Next October," Gilbert answered, feeling
a great many eyes turned upon him from
all directions.

"That is good," said the Professor, smiling again; "remember our college. We'd
be very happy to see you there." And
with this, he passed on, leaving Gilbert
rather bewildered, and rather uncertain
whether to believe his own ears. Just then,
to his infinite relief, Ray came pushing
through the crowd with a very happy face.

CHAPTER VII.

L OOK here, my dear fellow," said Ray, as soon as he •could get up to his friend, "my mother has come. She arrived this noon just as the exercises opened, and just too late to see me before them. Come into the parlor and see her."

"But the professors and doctors are all there," said Gilbert, "and 1 wouldn't like to go in, unless Mr. Winterhalter — "

"Oh," interrupted Ray, "but you're mistaken about that. The professors and doctors all went into Mr. Winterhalter's study, for I saw 'em. The parlor is full of other

115

people. Come on, for I told mother I was going to bring you."

Ray was so eager and delighted that he could not wait for Gilbert to decide, but tried to pull him along by the arm.

"You needn't hang back," said he, "for it's only mother you're to see, and she knows you already! How could she help it, when my letters have all been full of you?"

"But —"

"No 'but's!' You're to come right in without a word. When a fellow has been as smart as you this afternoon, everybody's got a right to be introduced and to have a shake of your hand. And when it's my mother — such a good mother, too — I think —"

"There," said Gilbert, "I'll go. I'd like to know her very much."

They followed at the heels of the crowd

that was pressing outward, and got into the hall at last; and after waiting till his patience was exhausted, Ray took Gilbert's arm and pulled him through the press into the parlor, which was very full of people. Most of them were parents and friends of the boys in school, and of course the scene was very lively and animated, and there was a great deal of bustle and chatting.

Ray took his friend down the long room, quite to the farther end, and stopped before a dark-haired, gentle-eyed lady.

"Mamma," said he, addressing her with a tenderness which Ray never used toward any one else, " this is Gilbert Starr."

Mrs. Hunter rose and took both of Gilbert's hands.

"Ah," said she, smiling very sweetly, " we are old acquaintances, though I never saw your face till this afternoon. May I tell you that I like Ray's friend very much already? "

Ray fancied himself to be the happiest person in school at that moment, and stood by his mother's side as she talked with Gilbert, feeling, somehow, very proud of both of them.

And when, a few minutes later, Gilbert bowed and took his departure, at a call from Mr. Winterhalter, Ray took the seat which his friend had vacated, saying,

" Isn't he smart, and handsome, and noble ? — and is he at all what you fancied him ? "

" Very much like," said Mrs. Hunter, smiling at her son's enthusiasm. " How could I help imagining correctly how he looked when your letters contained but little else ? "

" Well, really, but there wasn't much else to write about," said Ray ; " and, mother, are you satisfied with my rank ? Of course, I couldn't expect to beat Gilbert, and if I stand next to him, why — why —"

"Yes, I am satisfied," said the mother;
"satisfied with your rank, and satisfied with
your friend. Isn't that all you could ask of
me?"

"Yes," said Ray, gladly. "And are you
going to ask him to — to —— You know
what I mean!"

Mrs. Hunter put her hand upon Ray's
forehead, smoothing back the clustering
locks, and looking at him with the love and
yearning that make mothers' eyes soft and
gentle.

"Ah," said she, "what a great boy you
are getting to be!—growing away from
me, entirely. Almost of a man's stature,
and —"

But Ray quickly exclaimed, "Oh, no! I'm
just your own little boy, still," and put his
head down in her lap as he had been used
to doing when a child, and was so happy
and forgetful, with the dear hand stroking

his hair, that he did not look up for a long
time; and when he did, it was to find that
Gilbert had returned, and was smiling a
little at him.

Ray blushed, as if he had been caught
doing something very much beneath the
dignity of a young gentleman of his years.

"Why didn't you tell me Gilbert had got
back, mother?" he said, quickly.

"Well," said she, "I thought that as you
were 'still my own little boy,' it wouldn't
matter much."

Ray laughed. "Well, it's the truth," he
said; "I am!—and I dare say Gilbert would
do the same, if he had a mother."

"Of course!" said Gilbert, sitting down
beside his friends, and feeling, for the first
time, how very much alone he was among
all that gay company. It *would* be pleasant
to have a mother like Ray's to love him and
be proud of him; and should he be ashamed

to hide his head in her lap, or to have her stroke his hair? Not in the least! he thought.

Perhaps Mrs. Hunter fathomed his thoughts, for just then she said, " Ray tells me that you have no parents, and no home, in reality. May we hope that .you'll go home with us and spend the vacation ? " Gilbert was silent a full minute with surprise, and Ray fairly held his breath, waiting for an answer. Then Mrs. Hunter said, " You know, of course, that nothing could please Ray better, and it would be a great pleasure to me, too. So we really can't think of taking no for an answer, unless you have some very important reasons for an excuse."

How Ray thanked his mother for that! And presently Gilbert said, " Yes, I'd like to go very much."

" I declare ! " said Ray, jumping out of

his chair, " those are the best words, next
to the ones that made you head-boy again,
that I've heard to-day. You haven't the
remotest suspicion of the splendid times
we'll have! has he, mother?   Goodness
gracious! I wish I could express myself on
the occasion!"

" There's no need of anything further, I
think," said his mother. " Do you see how
dark it is getting? — and people are going
very fast. As it is quite a little walk to the
hotel, I think it would be better for me to
go, too."

" But you'll not walk," said Ray, " for I
shall order a carriage."

" But if there are none?"

" Oh, but I'll find one somewhere! They
can't all be gone, and if you'll stay here
with Gilbert, I'll go and look;" and he hurried out of the fast-darkening, and fast-thin-
ning room.

"Ray is a harum-scarum," said Ray's mother, "and I can hardly imagine how he came to attach himself to you, Gilbert," with just a hint in her tone at Gilbert's present graveness.

" Why ? " said Gilbert, with a quick smile.

" Well," she answered, smiling, " he is so very different, or was when he came under your influence. I think I have you to bless for a great change in him since that time."

" Why," said Gilbert, with honest surprise, " how can that be ? " And then, speaking out the next thought in his heart, he added, " I don't know how to guide or rule myself right, Mrs. Hunter, — indeed I don't! I'm only a beginner, and if Ray is any different than when we were first friends, I don't believe the credit is due to me at all."

He said this very earnestly, and Ray's mother knew he believed it. But she an-

swered, " You 're very frank, but I may see
some things which you do not. And it's
none the less true that you 've done Ray
good because you were not aware of having
done so; and Ray writes that to his mother,
which he would hesitate to reveal to you,—
just as he ought. Do you know that some
people's natures lead them to hide all their
deeper and more serious feelings under a
mask, as it were, of light and sometimes
even frivolous conduct? Did you ever
think that Ray might be one of them?"

Before Gilbert could answer, the subject
of their conversation came hurrying in, his
happy eyes beaming upon them both.

"All ready!" he said. "I knew I should
be successful. Now will you take my arm,
mother?" and as the gentle lady rose, Ray
added, "Good-by for half an hour, old fellow — while I'm gone to the hotel. I'll
come back and help you pack, for we start

at ten in the morning." And then, with a
last nod from them both, they passed out of
the parlor.

Gilbert sat down in the chair from which
he had risen as his friends departed, with the
new thought which Ray's mother had put
into his heart, fairly thrilling him. Had
he, all unconsciously, put better and truer
thoughts into Ray's heart by his own efforts
to become a better boy? Had this which
he had been trying to do for his own ad-
vancement in the right way, influenced Ray
so much that his mother could perceive a
change for the better in him?

The gentle lady's words — " It's none the
less true that you've done Ray good because
you were not aware of having done so,"
were very pleasant and grateful to him; yet
he could hardly persuade himself that she
was right. It did not seem as if *he* had
anything to do in the matter. " But," he

thought " if it *is* true, and all this long time
since I lost my captaincy and the fellows
cut me, Ray has been thinking of what he
ought to do and has been ' influenced,' as
Mrs. Hunter would say, for the better, — if
all this *is* true, I'll never take one more
thought about the captain's office or the
slights I get, or whatever may turn up to
trouble ! Good gracious ! how can I ? It's
just as if a fellow had been walking in what
he thought was a pretty uncomfortable path
for the sake of the right, and hot thinking
much else about it, when of a sudden it turns
out to be God's path which He has marked
out instead of one's self, and that one's
walking in it is not just for one's self alone,
but for those who are looking on, too."

And Ray, he remembered, was so light
and gay always, that he had supposed him
indifferent and unheeding. Yet, hidden under it all, was the earnestness and serious-

ness which she who knew him best, hinted of. .

Mrs. Winterhalter came into the room to see about lighting the lamps for the guests who were to spend the evening there, and spying Gilbert in his far corner, as she was about to go out, turned back and came out to where he sat.

" Are you down-hearted after such a brilliant examination as you passed this afternoon? " she asked, with some surprise in her tone.

" Oh, no ! " he answered, brightly; " I never was happier in my life. I've a great deal to be happy for, Mrs. Winterhalter, and it seems to me I never thought so much about it, as just at this moment. Do you think," he added in a lower tone, " that God ever marks out a path for one, and sets one walking in it without showing, at first, why it is done, or for what good it is done ? "

"To be sure I do!" she answered; "and what then, Gilbert?"

"Only — well, it seems to me that I've just found out that mine is one of His paths — I'm not certain, you know, but it *seems* so — and that I was set walking in it on others' account besides my own."

Mrs. Winterhalter took his hand silently, and pressed it in that tender way of hers which spoke so much more than words could have done, and then went out.

Gilbert looked at his watch, and saw that it was nearly time for Ray to return, and passed out of the parlor, too, in search of his protege.

The supper-bell rang before he had taken two steps in the hall, and as the boys passed toward the dining-room, Gilbert found Perry. and told him where he was going to spend vacation.

At first the boy's face clouded over; and

noticing this, Gilbert added, "I wish you were going, too. That's just the only drawback to the splendid time I'm going to have."

"But it needn't be," said Perry, brightening instantly; "for it's only two weeks that you'll be gone, and I can manage it pretty well, somehow. I'm glad you're going, Gilbert, and I'll bo at the station two weeks from to-night to meet you." At which brave reply, Gilbert was silent.

Ray was delighted to find the next morning a lovely one, — the sun bright on the river and its white sails, and bright over all the land. He took Gilbert off to his mother's hotel, long enough before ten, bidding him — "prepare to spend just the happiest, merriest, comfortablest two weeks you ever spent in your life, old fellow!" And Gilbert did.

Ray's home was much finer than anything

Gilbert had anticipated, but this was not what made the comfort and happiness which he found there. The gentle lady, whom Ray called mother, had most to do with it, he thought; and in the pleasant round of days that followed, she grew more and more like a mother to *him*.

CHAPTER VIII.

FEAR COMETH AS DESOLATION.

CAPTAIN PHILIP GATES was extremely mortified at the turn affairs had taken. He had stooped to a great meanness and wickedness, all to no purpose. It really seemed as if Gilbert Starr had been more successful and won more honors than ever. So, with a great storm of anger and mortified pride in his heart, that was all the harder to bear because he could reveal it to no one, he rushed away, as soon as the afternoon's exercises were over, to his chamber. He was confident that some one had proved a traitor, and therefore was not greatly as-

tonished when, on searching the place where
he had hidden Gilbert's packet, he found it
gone. The discovery, however, made his
heart beat very fast, and the blood rush to
his cheeks. Gilbert Starr had the advantage, now. He was at his mercy. " Oh,
why didn't I burn it ? " the captain thought,
regretfully ; " then there would have been
no proof ; Starr never could have recovered
it, and would have lost his place. Oh, why
didn't I burn it ? "

Regrets were quite useless, however,
and Gates sat down on the foot of his bed,
wondering what it was best to do. . Of
course, he thought, Gilbert would revenge
himself by disclosing all that had happened
to Mr. Winterhalter, and then disgrace, and
probably expulsion from school, would follow. The valiant captain had a good mind
to pack his trunk and leave school at once,
and so flee from the disgrace which Gilbert
Starr had the power to bring upon him.

"Oh, what a fool I've been!" Gates
thought, bitterly; "I've put myself right in
his power, and without doing him a bit of
harm, either; and now he'll have his revenge!" He remembered that Mr. Winterhalter was very strict concerning all matters
of honor, and, if he punished, it would be
with no light hand. And Gates knew that
his offence had not been a light one. "But,"
he exclaimed, with a burst of anger, "I
won't run away and give up to Starr without a struggle! I'll stay, if only to get that
sneaking traitor, Turner, punished! If it
hadn't been for him, all would have gone
well enough." And just then the door
opened, and Albert himself came in, bringing
his books and papers.

Captain Philip started up with very big
fists. "Oh, you traitor!" said he, advancing
in a threatening attitude; "I'll pay you for
this! I'll show you that you can't play me

such a two-sided game, without having to answer for it."

" Look here," said Turner, before his captain had time to strike, " it will be for your interest to. keep still. Strike me, and the whole story goes before Winterhalter."

" What's the odds?" said Gates, still threatening; " the story will go before Winterhalter, anyway; Starr will do that, and if I pound you I'll get part of my revenge, anyhow. So look out for —"

" Pshaw!" cried Turner; " you don't know Gilbert Starr. He won't take any notice of you, you may flatter yourself. He won't stoop enough for that. However, if you wish to pound me, you can make the attempt."

" I do!" said Gates, and would have carried out his intentions, had not the rest of the boys burst in with an account of how Professor Bainsley was actually stopping

in the crowd to talk with Gilbert Starr; and
those who were near enough declared that
they had heard the Professor say something
about Gilbert's going to college.

This was not at all soothing to Gates's
envious heart. It did seem as if everything
and everybody had conspired to praise and
exalt Gilbert Starr that afternoon.

"Oh, I hate him! I hate him!" he thought,
furiously. It is quite natural for a person
to hate one whom he has injured, and as for
Gilbert not noticing what had transpired,
Gates did not believe a word of it. He
judged his rival by himself, and as the captain was neither generous nor magnanimous,
he judged Gilbert to be destitute of those
virtues. Of course, he would revenge himself! Who would not?

The wretched captain sat upon his bed,
nursing his wrath toward Albert Turner and
Gilbert, till the supper bell rang. Then he

put on a very haughty expression of countenance and went down with the rest, thinking
to show Gilbert Starr that he defied him,
and all his attempts at revenge. But really,
this show of bravado was quite useless, as
Gilbert did not look once in the captain's
direction during supper, and when the meal
was over, went off directly with Ray Hunter. This set the captain somewhat at ease,
though it. puzzled him. Who ever heard of
such indifference? But after all, it might
be only an attempt to put him off his guard,
he thought, and Mr. Winterhalter might
send for him to come to the study at any
moment.. But the evening passed and no
such message came.

The next day — the first of vacation —
dawned, and an hour or two after breakfast,
Gates discovered that Gilbert Starr had
gone home with Ray Hunter to spend the
two weeks of recreation. Then his heart

gave a great bound of relief, and he began
to think that what Al Turner had said might
be true, after all.   And if it was true, Gates
thought, what a capital chance of revenge
Starr had neglected!   Really, it seemed
almost a pity to have such a magnificent
opportunity pass by neglected, even though
its improvement would bring ruin and shame
upon himself.

But before the forenoon had passed away,
Gates chanced to meet Mr. Winterhalter in
the hall, and the principal interrupted him.

"Now," thought the captain, with a shrinking at his heart, "your time has come, old
fellow!   But keep up a firm cheek,-what-
ever you do!"

But Mr. Winterhalter had only stopped
him to say, "Really, Philip, but we were
very much surprised and pleased with
that examination in mathematics, yesterday.
We'd no expectation of anything so brilliant.

Next term we shall look for great things from you."

Then he passed on, leaving Gates quite silent, and not without some sense of shame and meanness in his heart. But this feeling was only fleeting, and then he thought, joyfully, "The old chap doesn't suspect anything about it, so I'm all right! Really, I wonder if Starr was such a fool as not to know what an advantage he had of me?"

What do *you* think? — was it Gilbert's dulness and lack of perception that led him to pass by this opportunity for revenge, or was it — something else?

The two weeks of vacation passed very swiftly to those who spent them at home, but began to drag a little to those who were so unfortunate as to be left at Rainford.

Perry Kent was one of those to whom the last day of the second week seemed very long and almost unending. Never before, since the little boy's arrival at school, had Gilbert been absent a single day, and his present two weeks' absence was felt very keenly. The two weeks that were so short to his protector, seemed as long to Perry as the whole past term had been. Yet, in due course of time, Saturday night wore around, — *the* Saturday night which the boy had so long looked forward to, and it found him waiting at the Rainford station in the great crowd of travelers, and persons, who, like himself, were waiting for friends.

The constantly arriving and departing trains, the whistling, bell-ringing, bustle and roar of a great crowd, made such confusion, that Perry began to doubt whether he should find his friend at all. There were plenty of school-boys among the newly-arrived, and plenty of faces that Perry knew; and suddenly, while he was peering into the crowd, he felt himself lifted quite off the platform, and quite as suddenly set down again, and turning around, there stood Gilbert and Ray, both of them just as fresh, and bright, and handsome as possible.

" *So* glad to see you !" said Gilbert, taking his protege up again ; " how're the Winterhalter's school, yourself, and everybody else ?"

" First rate ! — and oh, what a two weeks it's been, Gilbert, — *so* long, *so* dull, and *so* tedious !" cried Perry, clinging fast to Gilbert's hand.

" Well, that doesn't at all agree with my two weeks," said Perry's protector, laughing. " Ray and I found them so short that we were actually puzzled to account for the time, and it doesn't seem much longer than yesterday, since we were here in the depot bound for a half-month of pleasure.

" Gilbert looked wonderfully refreshed and brightened up, Perry thought, and this quite

paid him for all the dullness and dragging
of the two weeks. Then they started homeward through Rainford streets, talking very
merrily, and thinking that, after all, it was
one of the dearest, pleasantest old towns
that man ever made,— especially just now,
when they were so glad to get back to it,
and the streets were full of light-hearted
school-boys like themselves, and the west
was shining like a topaz — so warm and
yellow and full of splendid light. And the
next morning they were hard at work over
their books again.

Hot weather came very early that summer. It seemed as if there had been a mistake somewhere in Mother Nature's calen-
dar, and that August had got substituted for
June. The last days of the month of roses
were fairly scorched, as if by the breath of
a furnace, and July came in hot and glowing,
and without a token of the much-needed

and long-looked for rain or showers. The grass began to wither and crisp, and Mr. Winterhalter's garden, back of the school-buildings, soon grew to look forlorn and disconsolate. The trees drooped, dirty and gray with dust, and all the land began to sigh for rain. But no rain came.

This unusual weather soon produced a perceptible effect upon study and tasks. Scholars grew listless and indolent, and lessons were but poorly learned or recited. Though the windows were wide open, the school-room would be very hot and suffocating, even during morning exercises; for there was no dew at night, and the great earth seemed to have lost all moisture or coolness, and the night-time was as sweltering as the day. It was very uncomfortable and oppressive, everybody knew, but as yet no one had thought particularly of danger.

One Sunday afternoon, Gilbert and Ray

with Perry Kent, had gone down to the
river's edge to catch a breath of fresh air,
if possible. They had a shady seat under
a low-hanging old apple tree, but as for
wafts of fresh air they were not to be found,
even there. Glassy, almost motionless, the
river lay under the burning sun. A sail or
two hung listless and becalmed over against
the opposite shore. The river-meadows, that
should have been green and rank, were
faded to a dull brown, and the whole wide
view, despite the sunshine, seemed very
cheerless and melancholy. Something of
this had touched Ray Hunter's bright spirits,
and for half an hour he had lain with his
head upon his arm, feeling very much depressed, and listening 'while Gilbert read,
"'Hide not thy face from me in the day
when I am in trouble; incline thine ear
unto me; in the day when I call answer me
speedily. For my days are consumed as

smoke, and my bones are burned as a hearth.'"

Then he broke his long silence with, "I say, Gilbert, doesn't that apply to these days? It seems to me that I never saw such a gloomy time, for all the sunshine and clear weather. It's worse than any cold can be, or any heat that I ever saw before. I feel just burnt up entirely."

Gilbert looked off the Book, across at the hazy hillside and at the burning, sluggish tide, and at last brought his eyes back to Ray. "I think David must have felt such parching heat and seen such a burning day as this," he said ; " else he never would have compared his affliction to them. But this is the way he comforted himself,— with thinking, 'But thou, O Lord, shalt endure forever ; and thy remembrance unto all generations.'"

" I wish we might do it,— as he did," said Perry Kent.

Before Gilbert had time to reply, Bob Upham came hurrying down the bank, quite interrupting their quiet. As he was one of Gilbert's old men, he was supposed to have cut his old captain's acquaintance, and so Ray was the first to speak.

" I wonder how on earth you can hurry ! " he said ; " it's more than I can do, comfortably, to keep still."

" But," said Bob, quickly, " there's reason to hurry. You don't know what's happened since noon."

" What has? " queried Ray, as a matter of necessity, and wishing that Bob would go away.

" Why," said the new comer, " Tom Fowler, Al, Gates, besides half a dozen in the under classes, are sick,— taken as suddenly as that ! Winterhalter had the doctor over from Rainford half an hour ago."

" What's the matter? " queried Ray, eagerly enough this time.

"Fever! and dangerous, too, the doctor said. There's plenty sick over in town of the same kind, and it's so contagious, that Mr. Winterhalter is going to call the school together at four o'clock, for all it's Sunday, and see what's best to be done. So I came down to tell you."

"It wants only a quarter of four, now," said Ray, looking at his watch as Bob walked away.

Then the two friends looked into each other's eyes for a few short seconds, both, doubtless, thinking of the danger that threatened. Ray spoke first.

"We might have known what would come from such a long, dreadful heat," said he, looking at the scorched meadows and glowing river; "and what will you do, Gilbert?"

"Go up to the house, first, of course," said Gilbert; "we can tell better when we've seen Mr. Winterhalter. Come, Perry!"

They walked slowly up the crisp, scorched lawn, Ray's heart getting very heavy. It had not been light and cheerful that afternoon, and now it was doubly oppressed.

"Oh, dear," he shivered, as they entered the school-room and saw the boys gathered in a deep silence, " it's all so sudden ! — and I can bear anything better than sickness."

To which Gilbert replied, " Pshaw ! don't lose your courage yet, Ray."

Mr. Winterhalter did not keep them long. He told them frankly that the fever was dangerous, and thought to be contagious ; that many people in the town were ill with it ; that he had not yet decided to close school, but those who were alarmed, or who wished to go home were free to do so on the following morning. And then he dismissed them.

There were but very few of the smaller boys who did not at once decide to start for home the next morning. Ray came to Gil-

bert, saying, " What are you going to do ?
It's time to decide."

" I've no home to go to," said Gilbert, " and
I do not think I should go if I had."

" But having no home need make no difference," said Ray, quickly. " Mine is yours,
too, and you know you'll be welcome.
Come, go home with me, and be safe."

But Gilbert shook his head. " I'll stay," ·
said he ; " I wouldn't like to run away. Perhaps I'd ought to stay — I don't know,— at
any rate I shall not go yet."

" Then I shall stay," said Ray, decisively.

But to this, Gilbert objected at once.   ·

" No, no," he said, " you must go home.
You're half sick already, but that good
mother of yours will make you all right in
no time ; while if you stay here you may
have a long illness and not half the good
care ! You must go home, Ray ! and I wish
I had half as good a place to send Perry
Kent."

"Look here," said Ray, with sudden fire, "that plan may please you first-rate, but it's a poor rule that won't work both ways. If you want me to go home you know what will send me,— nothing less than your consent to go, too. So that's settled !"

" But — "

Ray wheeled and walked away. "That's my decision," he called back; "you know what will alter it."

They, all the well ones, slept in the school room that night ; and the next morning there was a general rush for home. That day only one new case occurred, and this was Barry White, who had not felt able to leave with the rest. So school was virtually broken up, and upon the shoulders of the Winterhalters rested a great care and anxiety. The good lady's face — so weary, grave, and troubled — haunted Gilbert long after he went to bed that night.

CHAPTER IX.

GILBERT'S OFFER.

WITH the first sunbeams that stole through the slats of the shutters, Gilbert got up,— his first thought being of Mrs. Winterhalter's grave, weary face that had so oppressed him on the previous night.

It had got to be a custom with them all to look for signs of rain when arising, and Gilbert slowly pushed open the shutters, with little hope, however, of finding any such blessed promise in the sky, and looked out. Hot, molten, fiery, the sun was pushing up through some low-lying bands of smoke-colored clouds, and its red rays were beginning to travel over the parched earth,

and all the sky was set aglow with the
brazen light that had hidden its cool blue
for so many weary days. Afar, the hills
seemed ready to ignite as soon as the sun's
hot spears should touch them, and flame up
in a conflagration that might set the earth
a-burning. Not a waft of cool air greeted
him, not a trace of the dewy freshness and
fragrance of morning-time ; but parched and
stifling the new-born day came up to its
work with flaming banners and outriders of
hot and fiery garb, bringing death and evil
in their train.

Already the fainting fields had caught the
glow, and glared the same sickening color
as the sky. Gilbert closed the shutters to
shut out the hateful gleaming, and turned
away with a sigh. In spite of himself his
heart began to feel heavy and oppressed.
Just then Ray began to turn uneasily upon
his hard bed, and at last he opened his eyes

in a bewildered sort of way upon the un-
familiar surroundings of their sleeping-room,
and said, as soon as he had fairly made out
his whereabouts, " Are there any signs of
rain ? "

" No," said Gilbert ; " it's hotter than ever.
It seems as if the earth would catch fire and
burn up. The hills fairly smoke."

Ray drew a long sigh. Gilbert threw
himself down upon one of the benches, feeling very listless, and thinking that he felt
much like one of those parched, withered
fields that he had just seen glowing in the
sun. He heard Ray get up from his hard
bed and step slowly about while dressing,
and presently he was roused from a little
reverie by his friend coming and seating
himself beside him. Gilbert looked up at
his friend's heavy eyes and pale face, saying,
quickly, " Ray, you are half-sick ! You
oughtn't to be here another day."

" That's what I've come to see you about,"
said Ray ; " will you ● home with me ? "

" To help you on the journey? Yes, if
you 'll only go ! "

Ray's face fell. " No, no," he exclaimed,
" I mean will you go home with me and
stay ? I'm going to ask you this question
every morning till you consent."

If anything could have induced Gilbert
to consent, it was Ray's pale face and heavy
eyes. He took his friend's hand and fancied
it felt hot and feverish.

" You oughtn't to stay here another minute ! " he exclaimed, energetically. " You 're
a foolish fellow if you don't take the cars
and start for home this very morning."

" Very well," said Ray ; " you know what
will make me."

" Pshaw ! " said Gilbert, impatiently, " you're
unreasonable about it. I haven't decided
that I ought to go, yet. I'm head-boy, you

know, and though the Winterhalters never will ask me, I've been thinking that perhaps I ought to stay and help them through this trouble. They'll have their hands full, with all the help they can get, and I might do a great deal up in our room among the fellows."

" Good heavens ! " cried Ray, suddenly, while his eyes dilated, " you don't mean that—that you 'll go right into the fever ? "

" Why, yes,— if I took care of the fellows I should have to, of course."

Ray sat motionless for a few seconds, then got up and came to Gilbert, saying, while his voice quivered, " Please come home with me, old fellow."

But Gilbert was firm. He drew Ray down beside him, saying in his tenderest manner, " I thank you more than I can tell. You 're the truest friend a fellow ever had, but don't you see ?— you ought to go whether I go or not! You 're not head-boy, and you 're just ready to be sick, and there's nothing to keep you. And there's another reason why I can't go. I 'll never go and leave Perry Kent alone."

And Gilbert looked out to where his protege was sleeping, and colored at the bare thought of running away and leaving him to meet danger, and perhaps death, alone.

Just then the boy raised himself up and spoke, startling Ray and Gilbert, who supposed him sound asleep.

"But, Gilbert," said Perry, "you needn't stay one minute because I'm here. I want you to go and be safe,— indeed I do! Don't have me for a reason for not going."

Gilbert looked at Ray and smiled a little, and answered Perry with, "Go to sleep, little boy, and not trouble your head about us." Then bidding Ray to keep quiet, Gilbert went off to see whether there was to be any breakfast forthcoming. The house seemed very silent and deserted, and his footsteps echoed in a lonesome, hollow way, as he went down the hall to the kitchen. Mrs. Brant, the housekeeper, met him at the door.

"Breakfast, is it?" said she; "yes, it'll be ready, shortly. Mrs. Winterhalter hasn't forgotten ye, for all the dreadful times we're in. She brought down the orders for ye to have meals as usual. I'll ring the bell at meal-times just as always."

In going back Gilbert met Mrs. Winterhalter herself, with a tray of medicines. Her face brightened at the sight of him, and she set her burden down in a chair.

"It does me good to see your fresh face," said she, "after looking upon those up-stairs. You're quite well, and strong as ever?"

"Oh, yes," he answered, just as brightly as possible for her sake. "I never was better or stronger in my life. And how are they all up-stairs?"

The good lady gave a grave nod of her head, saying, "Not well at all. The doctor stayed as long as he could be spared from patients in town, but he looks very sober, and shakes his head whenever I ask for good signs."

"Have you plenty of help?" Gilbert asked.

"The under classes are well supplied," Mrs. Winterhalter answered, taking up her tray and preparing to go on, "and I wish I could say as much of those in your own room. We have one nurse there, but he can hardly attend to so many. I've been there myself, however, most of the time." And the good lady's face showed the effects of it.

"Now, Mrs. Winterhalter," said Gilbert, cheerily, and at the same time taking the tray from her hands and putting it back in the chair, "will you do me a favor?"

" Why — yes," she answered, surprised at his question, and still more so at his action; " and what is the favor ? "

" That you 'll let me go into the Club room for a nurse. The fellows all know me, and I 'm sure I could help a great deal,— running up and down for medicine and water and such things, if in no other way."

Mrs. Winterhalter's eyes suddenly welled with tears, and Gilbert was so surprised at this unusual sight that he cast his own upon the floor.

Then, taking his hand, the good lady said, with a slight tremor in her voice, " My dear boy, what shall I say ? You are very dear to us," and then she stopped to clear her voice which had suddenly grown very husky; then she continued, " Do you know, Gilbert, it might cost you your life ? " This was said with an effort.

" Of course," said Gilbert, now raising his clear gray eyes to hers," " there is danger

"My dear boy, what shall I say?"   Page 158.

of that; but I'm very strong and very healthy, — why, I never was sick in my life, Mrs. Winterhalter! — and I don't think the fever would take hold of me very easily."

She looked steadily at him for a moment and hesitated, — Gilbert knowing well enough that it was dislike to .put him in danger that kept back her answer.

"You needn't hesitate," he said, smiling; "I don't fear at all."

Then she said, laying her hand upon his shoulder, with a look upon her face that haunted him for a long time, — "I accept your offer. Come to me in the study after you've had your breakfast."

Gilbert said, "Thank you," and went on his way to the school-room, where he had left Ray and Perry, while Mrs. Winterhalter took up her tray and walked slowly upstairs.

Now this offer of Gilbert's, was not

so easily made as you may fancy. The
thought of so doing, had been in his heart
since that Sunday afternoon when first the
fever entered school. It was not at all
inclination that led him to make the offer,
for he detested illness, and could never
bring himself to endure the restraints of
a sick-room with any comfort. Every·vein
in his body thrilled with warm, healthy
blood, that demanded stir and action, and
could but poorly brook restraint or confinement. He knew that his self-appointed task
would be irksome and tiresome, and disagreeable, to say nothing of the danger that
lay in wait; but, with all this in prospect,
he had offered himself, and his services, and
Mrs. Winterhalter had accepted them.

He entered the school-room, looking twice
as cheerful as when he left it a half-hour
before, and said, cheerily, " Well, Ray and
Perry, we 're to have some breakfast just

as soon as Mrs. Brant's bell rings, which must be shortly. How are you, Ray? — any better than when you first woke up?"

Ray's eyes were a little brighter, as he answered, "Somewhat; but what on earth kept you so long?"

This was just what Gilbert would rather not have told; but thinking that the truth would have to be revealed soon at any rate, he answered, "Well, I've been enlisting, to tell the truth, — enlisting in Mrs. Winterhalter's army of nurses. I'm going on duty directly after breakfast."

Ray sat looking at his friend in blank hopelessness for a full minute. Then he said, with a sigh, "Well, I might as well bid you good by and go home, for if you once go into that room as nurse that'll be the last of you."

"Now you're beginning to talk sensibly," said Gilbert, with a brave cheeriness ringing in his voice; "go home, like a good fellow, and you'll be bright and well again in no time; but if you stay here,— well, you're not so sure of it by any means!"

"There, now you *don't* talk sensibly," said Ray; "and I *won't* go home. And," he added, with an attempt at his old mirthfulness which failed utterly and became dead earnestness at the last, "if you are going into that danger I'll like to stay till the last, and so not have you die up there quite alone."

Gilbert was glad to hear the breakfast-bell ring, and went out to the dining-room, thinking that Ray was outrageously obstinate; and Ray followed, thinking that Gilbert was very unaccommodating, and very reckless, and altogether an ill-behaved fellow. This kept them quite cool toward each other during the short meal, but when Gilbert rose to go to Mrs. Winterhalter's study, Ray relented and exclaimed, " Come back, old fellow ! Let's be friends till the last."

Gilbert came back, smiling and kind.

" You 'll be in better spirits, Ray, when I come back this noon," he said. " Keep up a stout heart, and don't worry about me. It's only doing duty, and that's what I set out to do, you know, last summer. It mayn't be pleasant, but it's right in my path, somehow," he said, shaking Ray's hands, " and — and I couldn't feel right to shove it aside."

With this he was gone, and Ray was left to wander disconsolately about the deserted school-room, and to make unavailing attempts to get a breath of fresh, cool air. Perry Kent came in, and Ray fell to talking with him about their common friend, and was surprised and not very well pleased, to find that the boy thought Gilbert's offer of aid a duty, which it belonged to him to carry out.

"I dare say," said Ray, with some show of indignation, "that you didn't try to prevent him from going in the least."

"No, I did not," said Perry; "Gilbert means to do his duty, always, and he wouldn't want me to hinder him, and I wouldn't want to."

"Well," said Ray, "it may be his duty,— I don't deny that,— but I think altogether too much of the dear fellow, to ever send him into danger. How would you feel if he caught his death there, and it was you who advised him to go?"

Perry Kent was silent, though not shaken in his faith of what it was Gilbert's duty to do.

Meanwhile, the friend of these two was installed in his new position, after being introduced to his companion, Stratton, who had been engaged as nurse for the Club room.

The room was partially darkened, and it was sometime before Gilbert could distinguish everything plainly; then he saw a sight that made his heart sink. Gates lay in one corner, Tom Fowler in another, and in the row between them were Al Turner, Barry White, and one or two who had been brought in from the second class's room.

Such a strong hold of them the fever had got, that they lay quite quiet, save an occasional muttered exclamation and whisper from the parched lips of one whose mind wandered in the vivid, but unreal, world of delirium.

The room could not but be close and oppressive, and Gilbert began to feel the closeness and the deep silence, at the end of the first half-hour.

But what was one half-hour compared with those that were to follow, and that did follow ?

That evening, as Mrs. Winterhalter sat at tea with her husband in the unwonted quiet that had fallen over the house, she said, soberly, and with a deep tenderness in her voice, " If anything was needed to convince me that there has been a great change in Gilbert Starr since last summer — a change that will grow and deepen with every day that passes over him — it has been more than supplied to me to-day. You remember that affair about the captainship of his company last summer, and how he was wronged and insulted? Well, when I saw how tenderly he cared for those very ones who wronged him, and who have not spoken to him since that time, nor of him, save in slander,— when I saw this, and how he was risking his life for theirs, I thought he had come very near to what the best of men come to but a very few times in their lives.

It made the tears come, and yet it made me very happy. I pray that God will spare him to us!"

"Amen," said Mr. Winterhalter.

CHAPTER X.

THE SHADOW OF DEATH.

OH, but those grew to be fearful days toward the last,— rainless, parched and scorching, and full of fear and death. Thick, smoky veils wrapped the hills about, and settled on all the far horizon, through which the sun rose up blood-red and sank away at night — hot and lurid.

The town was half-deserted. The fever had driven away all those who could flee to a safer locality; shops and stores were closed, and business had dwindled down to the trade which provision merchants drove; and of the throngs of drays and carriages that once filled the streets, all had vanished,

save the doctors' gigs which rolled by night
and day along the silent ways, and that slow-
moving carriage which bore the dead out to
the burnt, brown cemetery on Riverside.

The river shrank away, and sent up noi-
some smells from its black ooze to burden
the already stifling air. No clear, life-giving
breezes floated up from the sea. The
heavens were as brass, and the earth like hot
iron to the feet of men.

One night the bells cried out a wild alarm,
and a ruddy flame burst up into the night,
and glared over the stricken town, and into
many a window where the sick were moan-
ing and the happier dead resting; and there
were hardly strong men enough left to ex-
tinguish the fierce destroyer that threatened
by day and night. The smoke of this burning
settled down and wrapped the town in a
thicker, heavier gloom than ever. Oh, for
rain !— rain plentiful, powerful and saving !

There had not, as yet, been a death at Mr. Winterhalter's. Across the river, at Professor Roth's, two boys closed their eyes on one stifling night, forever; but at Mr. Winterhalter's they had had the best and kindest of care, and the most faithful of attention. Yet several lay hovering betwixt life and death, in a sleep that it was by no means certain they would ever awaken from.

Gilbert was at his post, a little worn and weary with the long strain upon his energies, but otherwise quite his own active, buoyant self. The fever had not harmed him, and he had not had a symptom of the dreaded disease, for all his long, close confinement. Ray had dragged himself around day after day, long after he ought to have been abed, and at last came to Gilbert one morning, with the fever shining in his eyes and burning in his veins.

"O, Ray!" Gilbert cried, as soon as he saw his friend; "what did I tell you?"

Ray was humble and penitent enough.

"I know!" he said. "I'd ought to 've gone,—I wish I had! But it's too late, now: and—and if I should get low, old fellow, I wish you'd send for mother. But don't unless I do, for she'd catch the fever."

He went to bed, and Gilbert watched him slowly sinking down into unconsciousness, as the rest had done, with a heavy heart. It seemed such a strange and fearful thing to get no answer whenever he called his friend's name, to receive no attention when he stroked his forehead and clustering hair, to be looked upon by Ray's shining eyes with no light of recognition in them.

This, and the sight of those white, fever-wasted faces about him, was what wore heaviest upon Gilbert's power of endurance. He could endure the physical labor and the fatigue of constant watching, better than the awful dragging of the weary days, full of sights and sounds that seemed to fairly burn themselves upon his heart, so that it was full of pain and almost despair.

Two or three days after Ray gave up, Perry Kent began to grow listless and heavy-eyed. Gilbert had been fearing it all the time, and detected the first symptoms of the coming fever in his protege. His face was almost despairing, as he went to tell Mrs. Winterhalter that the fever had fairly got a hold of the little boy. The good lady did her utmost to console him, saying,

"Very likely it will prove only a light attack, and soon over. I will have a bed made for him in the school-room, so that he can be quiet and comfortable, and where I can have an eye upon him, myself." This comforted Gilbert somewhat, but the boy's illness was another cause of fearfulness and anxiety.

Long, long days followed. Not a death

in the house, as yet, and the doctor thought there were some faint signs of mending, on the part of those who were first taken with the fever. Perry, to Gilbert's joy, did not seem to be very ill, though sometimes strangely stupid and insensible; and the boy had Mrs. Winterhalter's best care, and Gilbert was quite at ease about him. But poor Ray did not seem to mend in the least, and each day grew more wan and white, and more like the ghost of his former self.. Gilbert's heart grew heavy, and he thought of Ray's last injunction, and was in doubt whether to send for the gentle mother or not. He decided to wait a little longer,— just as long as he dared.

These were the hardest days for him. Good Mrs. Winterhalter saw how weary his face looked as he came down to his meals, which she made him eat in the study, instead of the great solitary dining-room, and never

failed to speak a word of courage and consolation,— real, hearty, vital words that did
Gilbert good. But she did not offer to release him from his post — how could she ? —
and he did not wish her to. He filled a
place in the sick-room which could be filled
so well by no one else, and help and aid
were scarcer than precious stones. She
could not spare his aid, and he never would
have accepted such an offer, could she have
made it. Whatever shrinking or despair
there was in his heart, not a thought of flee-
ing from his post found shelter there.

So the sun rose morning after morning,
and wheeled over into the west, and sank
through lurid vapor to its rest, and long
stifling, solitary nights followed.

On one of these evenings, Gilbert had
pushed open the blinds of the window by
Ray's bedside, and sat there, trying to feel
a cool waft of air upon his face. A little

light shone in from the west, just enough to reveal the white faces of the sleeping sick around him ; and upon Ray's countenance it fell, making it very pure and fair with its brown locks clustering all about it, like the angel's face in the painting which hung in . Mrs. Winterhalter's parlor.

Gilbert looked, tenderly stroked the white, unconscious forehead, and felt as if he should choke with pent-up tears. Ray die ? — pass away so young and bright and full of life into the great Hereafter? Die, and leave him alone ? He hastily put his own face down beside the unconscious one to smother the groan that came up. "O Ray ! Ray ! how can you die and be like a stone and lost to me ? He felt as if he wanted to get his friend in his arms and hold him back — back from the grave that he was slipping into. But when he had got quieter and remembered the uselessness of such giving away

to grief, and the need of keeping himself
as cheerful and buoyant-hearted as possible,
he turned to the window,— carefully turning the blinds so that the light might not fall
so squarely upon the face that he dared not
trust himself to look upon. Before him was
the dully-glimmering, half-deserted town, silent as those ruined cities of the past, where
only beasts prowl and bats flit. Silent, too,
was all the wide land, as if death had left
not an inhabitant therein. God's hand was
very heavy upon the earth.

But as Gilbert sat looking out upon the
desolation, the thought of what he had read
to Ray and Perry that Sunday afternoon
when first the fever came, flashed quickly
upon him,— the same thought with which
David had comforted himself in affliction:
"But thou, O Lord, shalt endure forever;
and thy remembrance unto all generations."
Though pestilence and death were on the

earth, God sat above all with love and care and remembrance that could never fail. There was comfort in the thought. _He_ was to endure forever,— never passing away, never failing, never forgetting. Whatever ruin or death darkened the earth, whatever trouble blasted, however thickly mists of evil and danger gathered, above all _He_ reigned — a mighty fortress of strength, immutable, and best of all, a tender Friend. Gilbert sat very quietly, with a strong sense of something _sure_ and _unfailing_ to cling to, making his heart lighter. It was _so_ good to know that the poor smitten earth was under Death's control only through the Lord's sufferance, and that it was not drifting through this terror of plague and death without a sure hand to guide it.

Just then, the bells struck out the hour in long-drawn, wavering tolls that echoed up and down the river, and over the empty

town. Gilbert heard the piazza-door open
and close, and caught a glimpse of the doctor's dim figure as he went across the lawn
to his gig. Then came some quick, but soft
steps along the lower hall and hurriedly up
the stairs, at which Gilbert wondered somewhat, as Mrs. Winterhalter's step had been
quite slow and weary of late. But she it
was, and she stopped to light the lamp in
the hall without, for it was very dark there.
Then she beckoned Gilbert to come out to
her, which he did. They stood looking at
each other for two or three long seconds, in
which Gilbert's heart began to beat very
fast, at something which he perceived in the
kind face before him.

"My dear boy," said Mrs. Winterhalter,
with a great effort to be calm, "can you bear
what I am to tell you?— even if — if it is
very bad news?"

"Oh," said Gilbert, suddenly, putting his
hand to his head, "do you mean — "

He could get no further, but stood looking
at her in such a bewildered way, as if he
had been stunned, that the good lady quickly took his hand, saying,

"Bear up, Gilbert. It's God's doing.
And you had better come at once."

He followed mechanically, holding on to
the balusters all the way down stairs, and
feeling so dizzy and shocked, that everything, at times, seemed to swim around him.
They passed softly into the great dimly-
lighted school-room, with the little white bed
in the center, and by which Mrs. Brant and
Mr. Winterhalter were standing; and they
were not any too soon. Perry had just
opened his great, clear eyes — all the fever
and delirium gone out of them — and at
once they rested on his old protector. Gilbert bent close over him.

"Oh," said the boy, very faintly, but very
delightedly, "*you*, Gilbert! You've been

gone a great while. May I get hold of your hand — just as I used to ? " Instantly Perry's hand was lying in his protector's, as it had so often lain in those bright and gladsome days of last summer. Perry smiled with satisfaction. " I 've been sick," he said, looking up into his friend's face ; " but I'm — I 'm almost well — now."

Gilbert's figure was shaking from head to foot, and it seemed to him as if he *must* cry out with the pain and anguish that were in his heart. Just then, Perry tugged a little at his hand, but said nothing,— only smiling upon his protector with such love and gratitude as no words could express. Then, after catching a little for breath, he drew a long, peaceful sigh, and was dead.

The truth did not reveal itself to Gilbert at first, and he stood — with his protege's hands clinging to his,— waiting for those clear eyes to open again. But chancing to look up, he saw the tears brimming Mrs. Winterhalter's eyes, and read the truth in her face. Shaking with his pent-up pain and grief, he dropped down upon the little white cot, and tried to smother the storm of sobs in the pillow. Mrs. Brant walked quickly away, and there were only the Winterhalters' left, and they stood a little way off till their head-boy's burst of grief had spent its first force. Then the good lady took Gilbert's hand and led him away — he struggling a little at the door to go back — to the study, and to one of the great easy-chairs. She tenderly smoothed his hair, sat by his chair a little while, still holding his hand, but said not a word to stop the great sobs that shook him from head to foot. Then she went away, leaving him alone.

What he endured here, in the quiet of the study, you may hardly know. It was his first heavy grief, the first time that death had taken anything that he loved, the first time that the wings of God's angel had ever brushed so near him, overshadowing his heart with its dark wings. And the stroke had come very suddenly and unlooked for.

When Mrs. Winterhalter returned, he was still sitting in the easy-chair, his hands hiding his face, and did not stir or look up when she entered. Putting her hands upon his head, she said in her soft, mellow voice, "'In my Father's house are many mansions: if it were not so, I would have told you. I go to prepare a place for you.'" Gilbert was silent, but the tears trickled down through his fingers. Then she said, her voice growing clear and steady with every word, "'And I will pray the Father, and he shall give you another Comforter, that he may abide with you forever;'" and again, "'I

will not leave you comfortless : I will come
to you.' "

" O, Mrs. Winterhalter," Gilbert cried
then, choking so that he could hardly speak,
" you don't know what the boy was to me ! "

" I do know," she said, soothingly; " he
was much nearer than a brother. You have
always been his protector, and there was a
different affection between you than exists
between brothers. His last smile gave you
unutterable thanks for it all." Gilbert wept.

" And since God has taken him to Himself," she continued, " we have no need
to weep. Perry's last breath on earth was
a happy one, and you have the thought to
comfort you that his last year was made
bright and pleasant by yourself. His happiness lay in your power, and you have kept
the trust well."

" It's not that — not he that I'm crying
for," said Gilbert, tremulously; " it's more

for my own loss, I think,— and that — that all those happy times are past, and I can never see him again, or — or hear him call me."

Mr. Winterhalter came to the study-door just then to call his wife, and she went away leaving Gilbert alone again, and this time to be undisturbed till the hot, lurid dawn broke over the land.

CHAPTER XI.

IT was well for Gilbert Starr that heavy duties and the wants of the sick prevented him from sitting down to mourn over his loss. The blow struck him heavily, and at a time when he was poorly prepared to bear it; it was good for him, therefore, that necessity compelled an immediate return to the cares and duties of the sick-room. So, on this sad morning, when the red light was sifting through the shutters into the darkened study, he began to sigh and shiver at the sight of it, remembering how the routine of weary watching and care must go on, for

185

all that a little figure lay silent and dead in the great lonely school-room.

It was a long time before he left the easy-chair in which he had sat that long, long night, and rose up with a determination to go back to his work which he knew had been left too long. It took all the energy and will of which he was possessed, to enable him to do this. He longed to sit all day in the dark, quiet study — away from all annoyance and all interruption, and have his sorrow and his mourning all to himself.

But as this could not be, he tried to put down this longing and go about his duty as he ought. But this was a hard thing to do. Then he remembered poor Ray, whom he had left so low and unconscious, and this recollection of his friend startled him into a quicker hastening from the soothing silence of the study. He came slowly out into the hall, and there met Mrs. Winterhalter look-

ing pale and worn, but with the placid smile
upon her face which always came there,
whether the face were fresh or tired.

"Good-morning," she said; "have you
rested at all?" But a look at Gilbert's face
was a sufficient answer, and she hastily
added, "But this will not do at all. You
must rest, or you will be ill. You had better go back to the study."

Gilbert longed to assent to this, but making an effort he said, "How can I? What
will become of Ray and the rest?"

"I will take your place," said the good
lady, cheerfully.

"No," Gilbert answered, resolutely, "I
will take my place — pretty quick. And —
and may I go into the school-room?"

Mrs. Winterhalter hesitated. "Yes, if you
think it best," she said at last; "but do not
stay long. When you come back, your
breakfast will be waiting for you, here."

And then, as if she thought Gilbert needed something more, she laid her hand gently upon his arm, saying, " Don't forget God, my dear. In Him is the strength,— nowhere else."

Passing on with lips that *would* quiver in spite of their owner's strong will, Gilbert left the good lady and entered the dim, shaded school-room. He went straight to the little white cot where Perry Kent lay. So calm, so still, so motionless — with the rare, grateful smile on his lips — with such unutterable peace expressed in every curve of the pleasant face, he lay, that Gilbert did not weep, but sat down, thinking that those two little feet had found a rest which was never to be broken.

It was not strange that he went back to that long summer day, when the little boy spent his first hour at school, and when he was thrown, in a manner, upon his protection. How Gilbert blessed that day! and how the tears ran down his cheeks when he thought of some which had passed since that time! Now they were all ended — the little life was finished — and he must go on without its cheery presence henceforth, forever.

So long was he gone, that Mrs. Winterhalter came tapping at the door, calling him, softly. Gilbert came out, his gray eyes abrim, and his lips pressed tightly together •to keep them still, and went into the study and made a show of eating breakfast, and then went up to his work, not having dared to trust himself to speak a word.

He came up to the sick-chamber with a heavy heart. Stratton, the nurse, met him with a sympathetic look and advised him to go back and take one day's rest, at least. But Gilbert was firm, and went up to Ray's bedside to be startled by something that was in Ray's face.

"Oh, Stratton," said Gilbert, quickly, "is he worse?"

The nurse knew what friends the two were, and tried to evade an answer. But Gilbert *would* know the truth, and Stratton at last confessed that the doctor had pronounced Ray very much worse. Gilbert looked as if he was going to sink down at first; then he rallied and said, "If that is so, I must telegraph. I promised him I would when he was first taken."

"But it will do no good," said Stratton; "and it's a long way to the office."

"Of course it will do *him* no good," said Gilbert, "but it may others, and I promised. Can you manage till I go and return?"

"Yes," said Sratton, "I'll try."

Gilbert hastily returned to the study, where the Winterhalters were finishing their breakfast. He found his hat — all the time keeping his face turned away from his friends — and started for the door. But Mrs. Winterhalter's quick eyes perceived that something new had occurred to disturb him, and followed to the door.

" What is it, Gilbert ? " she said.

Gilbert turned his white, despairing face toward her, as he answered, " Ray is worse. I'm going to telegraph!" and then hurried away without another word.

He was wise enough to take the road to town, instead of the winding river-path, for had he gone that way, every step would have been saddened by the haunting of a little figure, that once had traveled the grassy path, in eager haste to save him from doing a wrong. Even as he paced along the dusty, glowing road, the recollection of that splendid, crimson evening and all its many events, came vividly back to him. Now, there was no coolness nor fragrance in the earth, neither was there any little eager figure, and the crimson glare was the most hateful color that ever his eyes rested upon.

Sad and sorrowful he came into the streets of the stricken town,—his feet the only feet that made echo there. The telegraph-office was in a corner of the railway-station. Of course Gilbert remembered, as he came into the great building, how Ray, Perry, and himself had met there only a few short weeks before, and from thence walked home-ward in the amber evening-light, with no thought of what was so soon to follow. Now one was already silent under death's touch, and the other — Gilbert hurried into the office to rid himself of any more thinking about the matter.

The operator was an elderly man with a grave face, become so, perhaps, since the town had been fever-stricken, and almost his only duty was to send sad messages over the wires; but, as will always be the case when the heart is not a stone, this face had a sympathy and tenderness in it, that did Gilbert good.

" Your message," said this grave face, as if it understood all about Gilbert's hurry. Gilbert dictated it, gave the necessary directions, and leaned against the wall listening to the clicking of the instrument, while his own thoughts traveled much quicker than the lightning-flashed message to the far-off gentle lady, who was to receive it.

" Will you wait for a reply ? " said the operator, pointing to a leather-covered chair in the corner. Gilbert had not thought so far as this, but after a minute of reflection decided to wait, and sat down, feeling, for the first time, all his weariness and fatigue. People passed in and out — weary-eyed, sad-faced people, most of them — sending their ill-tidings and receiving replies. Gilbert found that his was not the only aching heart in Rainford by any means.

It seemed a long, long time that he had to wait, and as if everybody was more fortunate than himself in getting answers to their messages; and his heart and head ached so wretchedly that he put his face in his hands and tried to shut out the sharp, disagreeable clicking of the operator's instrument. He was presently aroused by a touch upon his shoulder, and then a scrap of paper was thrust into his hand without a word, and the operator walked back to his chair. With a gentle beating heart he read this:

"To GILBERT STARR, RAINFORD:

Ray's mother is ill,—cannot break the news to her. Do the best you can, and telegraph again to-night.

W. H. HUNTER."

It seemed to Gilbert as if everything had conspired to crush him down with evil news.

With his head fairly swimming, he got up
and walked blindly toward the door, and
there ran against Captain Forrest of the
Riverside school.

"Why," exclaimed the Captain, "is this
you, Starr? Good heavens! what ails you?"
Gilbert could not say a word, in spite of his
strong effort to do so, but stood looking
down at the stone steps through glimmering
tears. "You're ill!" said Forrest, making
Gilbert lean against him; "you oughtn't to
be so far from home in this fix. Have you
sent bad news, or have you just got some?"

"Both," said Gilbert, with an effort, and
standing quite straight upon his own feet.

"Oh, but these are dreadful times!" said
Forrest, quickly. "But we're getting better of the fever on our side of the river.
I've been through the whole of it, helping
take care of the fellows, but it hasn't
touched me, yet. So you have, too?"

" Yes," said Gilbert, mechanically.

" I thought so ! I knew well enough that
.you wouldn't run away, and that's partly
what put me up to doing *my* duty,— thinking of you at your post over on the other
side. But you 've been more fortunate than
we, for while you 've lost none, we 've lost
three."

" Perry Kent died last night," said Gilbert, wondering at his own calmness ; " that
was the first death."

Forrest started, exclaimed, " Oh ! " and
took a quick, sidelong look at Gilbert's pale
face, thinking, " Now I know what troubles
you. Poor fellow ! " Then, as there did not
seem to be anything more to say, and as
Gilbert was in a hurry, he took his departure, and left Captain Forrest standing on
the steps wishing that he had tried to say
something to comfort his friend.

Gilbert never could recall the events of

that homeward walk ; but he got there somehow, and feeling crushed and benumbed, took
himself up to the sick-chamber with the
message still crumpled up in his hand.

Stratton mercifully forbore to ask any
questions, and Gilbert went to his work of
giving medicines, bringing cool water and
fresh pillows, and when he had been his
round, sat down by Ray's bedside holding
his thin, white hand in his own. " Thank
God ! " Gilbert thought; " he can't suffer
what I do. He never 'll know that his mother was too ill to be by him at the last,— he
can't miss her." But if he should awaken ?
Gilbert was almost ready to pray that his
friend might die in unconsciousness, that the
mother's gentle presence and loving eyes
might not be keenly missed. He knew what
agony it would be for Ray to die without
seeing her. " O Ray ! O my friend ! — my
friend ! " he cried out in his heart. " What

shall I do?   O, God, help me! help me!—
teach me what to do!"

The forenoon wore away, and Mrs. Winterhalter came up to call him to dinner, fearing
that otherwise he would not come.   She
was much concerned at the haggard look
that had come into his face since morning.

"Gilbert," she said, resolutely, "this can
go on no longer.   We must try to do without your help up-stairs, for it's making you
ill!"

To which, Gilbert replied, "I wouldn't
leave now, for all the world.   I shall not
till it's all over with poor Ray.   Then—
then, it seems to me, I'd—I'd like to lie
down and die, too."

"Hush," said the good lady.   "Now I'm
going to lay you under commands.   You
shall have your dinner, and then lie down
for a two-hours' rest on the sofa in the study.
I will watch beside Ray, myself, and call you

if there is the slightest change for the worse." She did not ask him whether he assented to this arrangement, but, as she said, laid him under commands.

After he had eaten his dinner, and Mrs. Brant had carried away the things, Mrs. Winterhalter darkened the study, fixed the sofa-pillow most comfortably, and saw that her command to lie down was obeyed; and, though Gilbert did not suspect her presence, lingered till she saw that he was sound asleep.

The little study-clock, in striking four, awoke him. He started up, dismayed to find what a long time he had been sleeping. Then, just as if they had been waiting for a stir within, some one without the door tapped softly, and then entered. It was Mr. Winterhalter, this time.

"Ah," said he, as brightly as it was possible to look, "you are refreshed, I hope.

Mrs. Winterhalter says that Ray is no worse, and that you are to take a turn or two on the piazza, before coming up-stairs."

Gilbert wondered a little at this requirement, for the piazza was in the full, hot glare of the burning day, but complied, thinking there must be some reason for it, after all. And there was.

A great change had come across the sky. Gilbert felt it the moment his feet touched the piazza. The angry, crimson glare was gone, and a faint waft of cool air actually brushed his cheek. All the glowing, coppery haze that had filled the firmament, was changed to dun color, and hinted of rain. Feeling this delicious change, Gilbert sat down on the steps, rejoicing whenever a stray zephyr lifted the hair on his forehead, or cooled his cheek. Oh, if it might only rain! — only rain!

The clouds darkened, and against them

the town stood up in outline of roof and spire. Gilbert looked at it, thinking how many times he had seen the sun dip down and dye the whole like a city of gold, and feeling that the wide earth had lost something out of it that was most dear, and precious to himself, and that it could never be the same happy, happy earth again. .

From one of the tall spires — the spire of the church which all the school attended — a bell swung out a wavering, sweet clamor that lasted a few minutes — Gilbert paying little thought to it — and then, after it had been silent a little space, a long-drawn toll floated across the distance and seemed to strike right upon his heart, it came so suddenly. That was for Perry's first year. Before this sweet-voiced bell could strike again, Gilbert had stopped his ears and covered his face; then, thinking himself both weak and cowardly, he quickly took away his hands, folded them and listened.

There can be no voice more sweetly mournful than the bell which tolls out the years of a dear, dead friend. Every wavering knell strikes upon the heart and conjures up visions of the year for which it tolls,— some of them happy years, some full of content, others weary and griefful,— all of them making the finished tale of a life. So it was with Gilbert, as the bell in its tall spire counted sweetly out the thirteen years of his little friend; and at the thirteenth and last, he wept for very thankfulness, that he had made it a pleasant and happy one.

CHAPTER XII.

" O, RAY ! "

THE bell was still, and then, low down
behind the hills, a voice muttered —
hoarse and deep like the voice of a giant —
and dashing away the tears, Gilbert suddenly raised his head to listen. It was a long
time before it came again, but when it did
come it was vast and echoing,— the thunder-
ous, mighty voice of a storm, rising up from
behind the scorched hills.

For a minute he sat motionless, hardly
believing his own ears. They had all looked
and waited for the blessed tidings so long,
that now the news seemed too good to be
true. But puffs of cool, damp air floated

against his cheeks, and sighed through the
sad-hued, long-silent trees. A flash of fire
gleamed out of the fringed edge of the coming cloud, followed by a murmur of thunder.
There could no longer be any doubt.

Gilbert hastily rose and made his way
into the study. "There's a storm coming,
Mr. Winterhalter!" he said, with more
brightness in his face than there had been
in it for a long time.

"Thank God!" said Mr. Winterhalter,
throwing open the blinds to look out. Even
while he gazed, the echo of thunder floated
into the room.

Gilbert hurried away, up to the sick-room.
"There's a storm coming!" he exclaimed,
as he went up to Mrs. Winterhalter by Ray's
bedside, "and it will soon be here. And oh,
why did you let me sleep so long? You're
worn out!"

"No, no," said Mrs. Winterhalter. "You

were doing so well that I would not disturb you. Are you rested?"

"Yes!—and the storm! Oh, how can we be glad and thankful enough?"

"Now you talk like yourself," said Mrs. Winterhalter, gladly. And seeing how wistfully Gilbert was looking at his friend, she added, "Ray is no worse, but this is the crisis. Doctor has been here since you went to rest, and says that if he lives through this night, he will get well."

"O, Mrs. Winterhalter!" Gilbert cried, "is there as much hope as that?"

"Yes," said the good lady, slowly; "but I fear that, after all, it is but a faint hope. Ray is very low."

Gilbert looked at the wan face and pale lips from which all the breath seemed to have flitted, and sighed; and did not dare to hope that his friend would be on earth by morning-light. Then Mrs. Winterhalter went away, and as the hour for medicines had just passed, Gilbert had nothing to do but sit down by the window and watch the uprising storm and his friend's face.

Riverside hill was already under the sombre shadow of the cloud, against which its towers and spires gleamed whitely, and out of the blue-black heart of the vaporous billows that rolled up and surged one above another, little rills of glaring flame trickled down, followed by a great jar and crashing of thunder. Hill called to hill with voice of trembling depth, yet, to Gilbert's ears, as well as those of all the inhabitants of the stricken land, it was the sweetest, pleasantest sound which the whole summer had brought. Through the dust-choked, faded trees, the stormy breath of the cloud rioted, and raced in a whirlwind of dust up the road and over the parched country fields. Then a swift darkness settled over the earth, and then came — the rain !

Gilbert thrust his hands out to let the great drops fall upon them. He leaned far over the ledge that the blessed spray might fall upon his head. What joy was in the land! what rejoicing! for at last the Lord had remembered His people and His blessing had come down.

The great drops that heralded the coming flood, came thicker and faster, till all the air was gray with spray, and the landscape blurred and obscured.

As night came on apace, and the darkness deepened, the tempest — for tempest it had grown to be — did not abate. The rain came down like a flood. The earth shook with thunder as if the scorched, heated hills had at last ignited and burst asunder. The lightning flamed over the drenched land, and glared blue at the windows; and with the rumbling peals, the sharp, brittle crashes, and the steady, furious downpour, it seemed as if the earth was to be destroyed by the ravages of the elements.

The Winterhalters and Gilbert ate supper in the midst of this tempest, and, for all the fearfulness of the storm, were more cheerful than they had been for many a meal. They knew that with the return of moisture and coolness and verdure to the earth, the fever's power would be broken, and its progress stayed.

After the meal was finished, Gilbert said to the good lady who sat opposite, "If he should grow worse, and — and die, Mrs. Winterhalter, might I call you?"

"To be sure!" she said. "If there is any change for the worse, you must call us at once. I will come in at nine."

Gilbert took his departure, thinking of the telegram that Ray's father had bidden him send, but which the tempest forbade all hope of forwarding that night, at least.

"However," thought poor Gilbert, as he climbed the stairs, "in the morning the message will be a decisive one. He will either be dead or bound to recover."

How short the time seemed between this hour and morning-light, and yet what a great change was to take place! Either the angel of Death, or the angel of Life was to enter the house to stand by Ray's bedside. All this Gilbert thought of as he entered the chamber. The room had already grown purer and fresher, and with the shutters closed tightly, and the mild light falling on the quiet beds, it looked as cheerful and comfortable as such a room might.

Stratton had settled himself comfortably in one corner, ready for any call or aid, and thus Gilbert was left quite by himself in his corner by Ray.

An hour slowly ticked itself away, as he sat here in his chair, and after he had been

his round and got back to his post again, he
fancied that there had been a change in Ray
during his absence. It was not much —
only something in the breathing — and Gilbert could not tell whether it was a good
or bad symptom. His watch showed him
that it was already half-past eight, and remembering that Mrs. Winterhalter would
be in at nine, he decided to wait her coming.

The storm was at its height, and the crashes of thunder were fearful and numerous.
Gilbert's face was close to his friend's to
note every breath that he drew, and on the
pillow beside him, the watch lay ticking
away the minutes, and, as Gilbert began to
fear, Ray's dear life, too. As he looked at
the passive face, the quiet tears filled his
eyes, and he thought of the place he was
in — watching out the last swift minutes
of his best friend — with wonder at his own
calmness and endurance.

Just then heaven and earth seemed to
come together in one prolonged, fearful,
hollow crash, and Gilbert turned his face
to the window, half expecting to see the
walls totter or light up with flame ; but as
the echoes died away, and the walls stood
firm and unscorched, he turned back to the
pillow, and as he did so came near crying
out, for, clear and undimmed, Ray's eyes
were looking at him.

Gilbert's first impulse was to shout for
very joy ; but remembering himself, he bent
his head low and kissed his friend's lips, and
laying his head beside the dear one on the
pillow, sobbed softly, and behaved in a manner altogether unusual for Gilbert Starr.

The angel had come, and it was the angel
of Life ; though Gilbert was not so sure of
this fact, till some time after. He remembered too well how Perry Kent's eyes had
opened — in this same calm, clear manner —

at the last. So, without daring to take his eyes off Ray's face, Gilbert made signs to 'Stratton, and asked him to go for Mrs. Winterhalter, without an instant's delay.

The nurse complied, and two or three minutes after, the good lady came in. Gilbert pointed to his friend's face, without a word, and stood watching Mrs. Winterhalter's countenance.

" Well," said he, after she had felt Ray's pulse and bent over him for a few seconds, " is it for good or bad ? "

" I think it is for good," said she. How those words thrilled Gilbert !

" But," said he, not wishing to hope when there was no hope, " I am afraid that it may be like poor Perry's waking, after all."

" No," Mrs. Winterhalter answered, " it is not at all like that,— except that he has wakened out of a long sleep."

Gilbert sat down, perfectly still with his

unutterable joy. The kind lady staid till half-past nine, and as there was no change for the worse, rose up to go, saying, "The crisis must be past, and he certainly seems a great deal improved."

"And shall I do any differently than before?" Gilbert asked.

"No; keep on just the same, and at five the doctor will be here," Mrs. Winterhalter answered, and went her way with a lighter heart than she had had since the first day fever entered school.

Gilbert thought no more of storm or peril that night, nor did he close his eyes in sleep. He was much too happy for that. His gladness and gratefulness could not be expressed. If he seated himself a little way from the bedside, thinking to take a few minutes of rest and perhaps sleep, he was presently filled with such a desire to go back and look in Ray's face, and assure himself that his friend was really wide-awake and breathing stronger with every breath, that sleep and rest were out of the question.

No matter if Ray was too feeble to talk or stir,— the precious life was left, and it could be brought back to its former robustness by care and the tenderest attention; and no care, Gilbert thought, would be too difficult or irksome to bestow upon his friend. No matter if this friend had come back to consciousness weak and faint as an infant, and with not half so strong a hold of life ; life had been spared, and this life was Ray's ! So all the happy, grateful night he kept vigil — too glad to sleep, too glad to think of his fatigue — and when the gray dawn broke over the drenched land, he knelt down by the bedside to pray for himself and Ray, and to thank God again and again for this friend that was dead but now was alive again.

The thunder-storm had turned into a settled rain, and all the day was gray with a
steady pouring; but Gilbert contrived to
get a message to the telegraph-office through
the doctor's agency, and thus sent the good
news flashing to Ray's friends. About
nightfall a messenger came down from the
office with a reply. It only said:

"God bless you. Ray's mother is not
dangerous — will be better soon. Send
word if there is a relapse.

W. H. HUNTER."

Gilbert put the strip of paper away for
Ray to look at as soon as he should be able,
and felt that he had a double reason for being
glad and happy. There was only one thing
lacking now, and that was the pleasure of
hearing Ray's voice once more. He did not
care whether it was clear and firm, or only
a faint, husky whisper, so it but came. And

one morning, a day or two after this, the much wished for pleasure was his. The storm had cleared away and left what seemed like a new earth. The air was clear as crystal, and the sky blue and pure as a sapphire. Already, along the path-edges, the grass was sprouting green and fresh, and afar the fields began to flush anew with the tender color of spring-time.

Gilbert had the blinds wide open and the window up, for all the patients in the room were better, except Gates, and as he was filling the glasses with fresh water, Ray awoke from his long night's sleep, and said, the first thing, " Gilbert."

Gilbert came near dropping the pitcher, and was by his friend in an instant.

" O, Ray ! " said he,— " just let me hear you say that again."

" Gilbert," said Ray, putting out his hand, and smiling for the first time.

Ray's friend thought himself the happiest fellow in Rainford at that moment, as, indeed, he was.

By degrees the feat of asking a whole question was achieved, and for every question that Ray asked with his tongue, three were asked by his eyes, and Gilbert soon got so as to divine his friend's wants and wishes quite readily. Stratton stared very hard, sometimes, when he heard Gilbert answering questions which, so he thought, had never been asked.

Now Gilbert would have liked no better pleasure than to sit beside Ray all day long, but just at this juncture, Captain Gates's illness began to be a serious matter, and the care of him a somewhat difficult task. He was delirious, and the fever had not been heavy enough to greatly reduce his strength, so that Gilbert and Stratton often had all they could do to keep the captain in his bed.

One by one, just as soon as they were able, the other convalescents were removed to the quieter school-room, where there was more room, and they could stir about a little. But Ray, who was not yet strong enough to bear removal, and Gates, who did not mend at all, still remained, and between the two Gilbert's time and care were divided. However, there was prospect of release ahead, as the invalids were recovering so fast, that Stratton would soon be enabled to leave them altogether and devote his time to the Captain, and then — O happy moment! — with duty done, and Ray almost well, and unbroken leisure and rest his own, Gilbert was sure that he could drive away the aching and lassitude that, unknown to all but himself, had of late oppressed him.

One evening, when Gates had got quiet, and with the blinds and window thrown wide — letting in a great flood of radiance

from the golden-hearted west, that fell across
Ray's bed, making him look more than ever
like the fair-haired angel in Mrs. Winterhalter's painting — Gilbert sat in his chair, answering his friend's eager questions which
had been waiting for a leisure moment all
the afternoon. Ray had been over the
whole account of the good news which his
letter had brought him that night (his mother was coming to see him) and now was en-
quiring after his classmates.

Gilbert had just said, in answer to Ray's
query, " Gates is no better to-night. I wish
you were able to be moved below. You'd
improve a great deal faster. All the fellows
down there are doing wonderfully well."

" Oh," said Ray, looking at Gilbert with
his calm, gold-touched face, " that makes me
think ! Where is Perry Kent ? "

There was a dead silence. Then Gilbert's
breast heaved, his chin quivered, and the

quick tears flashed into his gray eyes. " O Ray ! " he said, tremulously.

" There, there, — don't ! " said Ray, quickly, touched, and quite shocked at the revelation.

This was the end of all questions for that night, and Gilbert's little friend was a tacitly forbidden subject for a long time after that ; though when Gilbert brushed near the bed, after lighting the lamp that evening, Ray put out his hand to press his friend's with silent sympathy, that was much better than any words.

CHAPTER XIII.

WHAT FOLLOWED A TUMBLE.

THE power of the fever was broken, and its progress stayed throughout the land. The fields grew green, the earth put off its scorched garments, and once more the river rolled broad and blue down to the sea. People came back to their homes and their work, and again life and labor went on in their old channels. The sails came up from the sea, the drays rumbled and rattled along the shadow of Riverside, and once more Rainford streets were noisy with the hum and stir of business. Only the cemetery, nestling with its firs and white slabs on the hill-slope, hinted of what had been.

At Mr. Winterhalter's the invalids were
creeping out into the cheerful, happy freshness of the summer days, rejoicing in their
life and liberty. Captain Philip still hovered
between life and death, and as the remainder
of the class were now in need of little care,
Stratton took Gilbert's place by Gates's bedside, and at last he was at liberty ! But the
hour of release came too late. The strain
had been too long and severe for even Gilbert's sturdy frame, and with a sudden snap,
as it were, of all his powers of endurance,
the climax came.

He was coming out of the sick-chamber
one morning, and as he took the first step
towards descending the stairs, a swift blind-
ness and dizziness came upon him, and that
was the last he knew for three long weeks.
But the inmates of the lower floor were
startled by a dull fall and tumbling, and Mrs.
Winterhalter rushed out of the study with

a white face, to find Gilbert Starr lying very pale and still at the foot of the stairs, while the blood — not from any vital part — but from his nose, which had been sadly bumped in the sudden descent, trickled along and under the hall-mat. Of course, good Mrs. Winterhalter was very frightened, indeed. For half a minute she stood motionless, thinking Gilbert had broken his neck, at least; then she cried for help. Stratton, who had heard the tumble, came running down from the sick-chamber, and Mr. Winterhalter, who had heard nothing but his wife's cry, came running too, and quickly there was quite a crowd gathered at the bottom of the stairs, all frightened and dismayed at the sight that met their gaze. Mr. Winterhalter recovered his senses sooner than the others, and got Gilbert's coat and vest open, and his hand upon his heart.

"He is not dead!" he cried; "Stratton, help me lift him."

They took him up tenderly and carried him into the adjacent study. Here, upon the sofa, and after five minutes of exertion on the part of the Winterhalters and Stratton, Gilbert began to breathe, though only faintly.

"He must have swooned at the top of the stairs," said the principal, "and from there rolled to the foot."

"I thought he looked pale when he started to go out," said Stratton, "and I believe he said something about wanting a breath of fresh air; but he has looked so before, so I didn't mind."

Fortunately the doctor came in just then to see Gates, and Mr. Winterhalter brought him into the study at once.

"Ah!" said the physician, as he seated himself by the sofa. "Well, I've been expecting it."

"Expecting what?" said Mrs. Winterhalter in alarm.

" He must have swooned at the top of the stairs "   Page 225.

"Just this," said the doctor. "He's worn out.. I knew it would come with a snap when it did come."

" Do you mean the — the fever? " faltered Mrs. Winterhalter, looking ready to faint away.

"Yes, madam," the doctor answered in that suave, bland tone so peculiar to the profession.

The good lady sent the crowd of eager faces at the door back to their own province.

" Let him have plenty of air and light," said the doctor, as he rose to go ; " I 'll come again at noon."

After the door had closed behind him, and they had heard his boots go squeaking up-stairs, the husband and wife sat looking in silence at each other for a little space. Then Mrs. Winterhalter, looking at Gilbert with a sad face, said, " Poor fellow ! "

" Where shall we put him? " said the principal.

"Here," the good lady answered, quickly; "he shall stay here. I will have a bed put up in that corner by the big book-case, where I can care for him myself. No one else shall do it."

"Are you not too much worn?" suggested her husband.

"No!—not to take care of Gilbert. Do you remember all he has done for us, Mr. Winterhalter?"

Mr. Winterhalter *did* remember. He called Mrs. Brant and assisted her to make up the cool, snowy bed, where Gilbert was to lie, and then, by dint of Stratton's help, removed the ex-captain's clothes and got him down among the pillows at last. And that was the beginning of a long sleep,— tired, worn-out nature asserting her rights, and taking a deep, unbroken rest. Slowly but surely the fever had fastened upon him, working insiduously and undermining his vitality all those many, fearful days when he sat among his stricken comrades, and now here was the result.

No sooner had Mrs. Winterhalter seen that Gilbert was comfortably installed in his new quarters, than she bethought herself of Ray, and went out into the school-room — devoted to the use of the invalids — to find him. He was sitting by a window, and cried out as soon as she entered,

" O, Mrs. Winterhalter ! what *has* happened ? The boys won't tell me."

" We thought it would make him worse or something," said Tom Fowler.

But the good lady knew that the truth was better than suspense, and answered, " Gilbert fainted away, and is going to be quite ill, the doctor thinks. But we have him nicely settled in the study, where I can be with him through it all."

Ray's face was rather shocked, but he tried to be brave. " I 'm glad you told me,"

he said, "for I can bear it a great deal better than imagining all sorts of things. I'd
like to get well and help take care of him!
And — and might I go in and look at him?"

"No," said Mrs. Winterhalter, shaking her
head, "that would not do at all. You must
not expose yourself. Try to be patient and
wait till he's recovering." And with this,
though it was a very hard thing to do, Ray
had to content himself.

Now, in one sense, if not in all, Gilbert's
sickness was a blessing in disguise. It
brought all those hearts that had been set
against him back to the love and loyalty of
the previous summer; only, as before the
loyalty grew out of admiration, now it
sprang from a deep, fervent sense of gratitude and affection,— a loyalty that could not
be shaken because it grew out of something
real, deep and vital. How could Gilbert's
old men — as one by one they crawled up to

their former strength and robustness — keep their hearts steeled against the remembrance of all that he had done for them? They could not; they did not try. They gave him at once, without question or hesitancy, all the fervid gratitude and affection of their hearts. " Greater love hath no man than this, that a man lay down his life for his friends." Gilbert had not yet parted with life for their sakes, but was he not now very near it? Had he shunned the danger in the least to keep his life? Had he not the same as laid it down for them? — they, who had scorned him for a weak, soft-hearted, unmanly fellow!

Well, it is not the greatest or noblest deeds that *seem* greatest or noblest at the time of their performance. Deeds which seem very insignificant and are pushed away into the darkness and forgetfulness of to-day by more startling and fortunate claimants for admiration, may, in the far-off to-morrow, be the deeds most honored and most revered.

So, when . Gilbert perilled his life for his enemies, and was not conscious of doing any particularly noble act, this very unconsciousness and forgetfulness of self, served to make the lesson a deeper one and fuller of the beauty and grace which rest upon all noble acts. Truths strike all the deeper and take firmer root, for flashing upon one in their own full beauty and significance, instead of being hammered in by somebody's mallet; and the act which had done so much for Mr. Winterhalter's boys took a fairer, lovelier shape in their eyes now that its nobleness dawned upon them day after day, while their benefactor lay wasting under the fever which he had taken from them. They thought of Gilbert's deed, and talked of it with awe and wonder in their tones,— because, you see, they could not conceive how

it was possible for him to do so much for
those who had wronged him.

They beset Mrs. Winterhalter every half-
hour to get tidings from the study where
their old captain was locked in the death-
like fever-sleep ; and if the news was good,
they said, " We'll have him back again
pretty quick, and won't we be kind to the poor
old fellow ! " but if it was bad, they went
around with very sober faces, thinking, " Oh,
if he will only get well so that we can tell
him that we *know* he isn't a sham, or a
traitor, or anything but what's a hundred
times better than we are ! "

This great change in Gilbert's enemies
both touched and pleased Ray. " It's come
— the change — just as Mrs. Winterhalter
said it would," he often thought to himself ;
" but oh, how much it has cost the poor fellow ! — and there's no telling that he'll ever
get better to know that everything has come

right at last. But if he don't — Well," Ray would think, almost choking with tears, " I suppose he 'll know it all when he's dead, and gone — like Perry Kent — to heaven."

They passed the evenings — these invalids — in such amusements as were suited to their yet weak limbs, playing backgammon, chess, and the like ; but there was generally a little space before going to bed, when the chess-boards were pushed away and they sat chatting, for comfort and consolation, among themselves.

One evening Mr. Winterhalter had been in, as usual, to tell them how Gilbert was progressing, and as the news was unfavorable, they all sat silent and depressed, after he was gone, till Tom Fowler burst out with,

" I say, I wish somebody would speak ! I can't stand this. It's worse than being downright hard sick — a great sight ! "

" What can we say ? " Ray asked, mournfully.

"Something!— I don't care what," said Tom; "I'd rather talk about the poor captain than sit so dreadfully blue and lonesome. Oh, but I tell you, boys, if I could get rid of thinking of some things that torment me, I'd give all the money I ever had or ever expect to have."

"What troubles you?" said Al Turner.

"I should think *you'd* better ask that," said Tom Fowler, almost bitterly; then changing his tone, he added, "Well, it's no time to be bitter, and I won't be! We were all to blame. We knew perfectly well that we were doing an outrageous thing when we took the poor captain's command away, and treated him shamefully for saying his prayers like the man he was, and doing what he thought was square and right about that flag. I declare, I don't know what a lot of fellows won't do when they're mad!"

"And to think what we put in his place!" said Barry White.

"I know!—that—that—Well, I won't
call poor Gates names, now," said Tom.
"But that's not the worst!—it's to think
how we insulted the poor old captain every
chance we could get, calling him names that
belonged to ourselves instead of him. I
remember·one Sunday when we came upon
him down by the lawn-edge, and did our best
to disturb him.· By and by he got up with
his Bible in his hand—we'd made such a
clatter that he couldn't read—and just then
says I, as he went walking away, 'Behold
the just man made perfect!—the *good*,
meek, devout hypocrite who walketh squarely, singeth through his nose, and looketh not
upon sinners.' With that he wheeled around
like a flash, his eyes fairly snapping—you
know he's got a hot temper, and it used
to fly up like a rocket—and there he stood
looking at me, his hands twitching, yet without saying a word, till his face all softened

down as kind and gentle as a woman's, and great *guns!*" cried Tom, bringing his hands together with a clap, "I was so ashamed of myself that I was ready to creep into a knot-hole, though of course I blustered and pretended it was all a good joke. I never forgot that. And now, only last night, I dreamed the poor old fellow had got well, and that we all went in to shake his hand —as I hope we shall do before long—and when I asked him to shake hands and forget old scores, he only looked at me with that same gentle face which he had that Sunday, and kept back his hand. I don't know what ails me, but I've kept thinking of that dream ever since, and it seems to me, boys, that if I could be sure that he wouldn't keep back his hand when the time really does come to shake it, and that I could be *certain* that he'd forgiven me, if he should happen to go away without being able to tell me so

—I'd, I'd — oh, I'd give one year of my life! and that's something for a fellow that likes to live as well as I do."

Tom had to wink very hard during the latter part of this long recital, to keep the tears back where they belonged, and when he had finished, five long minutes ticked themselves away before anybody spoke. Then it was Ray.

"Tom," said he, huskily, "I thought you hadn't much heart, but — but I don't think so, now; and I can tell you just as certainly as if I had it from the dear fellow's lips, that he never will keep his hand back, and that you are forgiven. Would he have taken care of us all with his heart full of hate and dislike?"

There was no need of answering this question, and in words it was not answered; but in their hearts — Ah, hearts, are often too full to let the tongue speak.

CHAPTER XIV.

THE crisis of Gilbert Starr's fever came at last—and passed. Weak, wasted, and more helpless than a little child, he once more opened his eyes to light and life, and a glimmering consciousness of friends who flitted about his bedside, bestowing the kindest and tenderest of care.

It seemed to him, now, as if he had been locked in a long, deep sleep, and that this present half-consciousness was the lighter slumber of a dream, and the moving figures and the dim, far-off voices but the unreal sights and sounds of dreamland. This half-stupor lasted for several days; then he began

237

to take a stronger hold of life and waken out of his long slumber and dreaming.

A bird in the syringa bushes, just without the study-window, awoke him one morning with its singing and chatter, and to Gilbert it seemed as if the bird had come on purpose to waken him to the brightness and heartiness of the life from which he had been so long shut out, for both head and heart were lighter and more alive to outward things than they had been for many a day.

Very slowly his eyes opened to the pleasant, shaded light of the room, and took in the figure of some one sitting on the bed-edge,— a figure which seemed very familiar, and whose presence made his heart beat warm and quick; but who was it?

Gilbert's efforts at thinking or reasoning all resulted very unsatisfactorily,— one thought seeming to chase another in endless

pursuit through his puzzled head; and so
he was obliged to lie tranquilly regarding
the silent figure that stirred not from one
half-hour to another. Though the poor fellow's head was too weak to tell who it was
sitting so patiently beside him, yet he was
glad to have the figure there. Once it
stirred a little, and seemed about to depart,
and he struggled to cry out and bid it stay;
and, though his tongue made not a sound,
the figure seemed to understand, for it settled down into its old quietness.

You will think this was a strange predica-
ment for lithe, agile Gilbert Starr to be in,—
too weak to talk, or think, or put out his
hands,— and so, you may be sure, it seemed
to his friends and the patient figure sitting
beside him. They had always known the
ex-captain as the sturdiest, healthiest fellow
in school,— never sick, never ailing, and full
to overflowing of stir and spirit. Now, to

see him lying white and ghost-like, without power of speech, or even thought, and unable to move his own limbs, made the tears come when ever they thought how near he had been down to the very gates of death.

Pretty quick Gilbert saw this figure beside him put out its hand. It rested gently upon his forehead, and its touch was so grateful that he closed his eyes for very pleasure and drifted away into sleep. When he awoke the figure was gone, and a shaded lamp was burning in a corner of the room; and some dim consciousness of the fact that it was now night, and that he had been asleep a long time, struggled in upon him. Then a figure of different shape drew near, treading softly, looked at him, went away, and presently returned with some gruel and broth which it proceeded to pour down his throat by teaspoonfuls. Then the figure went away, and after a few minutes of

watching the lamp, he drifted back into the
mysterious world of sleep. So, you see, the
" poor, old captain," as Tom Fowler called
him, was little more than an oyster,— taking
in food and nourishment, but giving little
indication of life, or sense, or motion. But
he got a little stronger hold of human things
every day, and the next morning, when he
awoke, it was to find the pleasant figure
sitting beside him, and to make a renewed
effort to discern who it might be, and, if he
should be so fortunate, speak its name.

It was an hour before anything like the
truth began to dawn upon him; but then,
quite suddenly, this little word — in the
shape of a thought — flashed upon him,
" Ray ! "

Gilbert lay very still (that was not so
strange, seeing that he could not stir) and
very happy (because of the truth that had
found its way into his poor, weak head) and

then he strove to make a sign that should show his friend that he was aware of, and rejoiced in, his presence. Another hour passed before he had accomplished anything toward this; but, after at least fifty failures, there struggled from his mouth one little sound — a faint, whispered, tremulous " R."

The effect of this sound upon the figure was quite astonishing. It bobbed about, and showed signs of the most extravagant joy, and to end off with, put its head close down to Gilbert's own, nodding and smiling approvingly. Thus encouraged, Gilbert made another essay, and after a long and almost despairing struggle, whispered, " A." At this, the listening figure went into ecstasies, and raised one finger to signify that there was yet one letter wanting. Gilbert understood and went to work to pronounce it; but it was no light matter and when at last the feat was achieved and he had actually spoken R — A — Y, he lay quite weak and exhausted. But the figure was so de-lighted at this achievement that it ran away and presently came back with another, and the two bent over the ex-captain with faces full of delight and gratitude.

In this feeble manner Gilbert Starr strug-gled up toward his old hale, hearty life, getting the most faithful of attention from Ray Hunter, and as tender care from the Winterhalters as if he had been their own son; and getting a clearer consciousness of things every day, as well as a better con-trol of his own powers, it so happened that as Ray came in to his pleasant task one morning, Gilbert looked up and said, as plainly as possible, "Ray!—good morn-ing!"

Of course there was great rejoicing, and Ray had to go back to the school-room to tell the fellows there that, "Gilbert said 'good morning,' just now, like a book! — and he looks bright enough to chatter like a magpie;" which Gilbert did not do that day at least, though he managed to articulate a few questions. But the next day he was so much better that questions were no rarity at all, and Ray sat beside him, unspeakably happy.

"You can't know, old fellow," said he, "how I feel to hear you talking bright and chipper again."

"As if I hadn't been in the same place," said Gilbert.

"Not quite in the same place," said Ray, shaking his head; "there's some difference between my getting well and yours. Oh, but we thought we 'd lost you more than once, old fellow ! "

Gilbert felt as if he had been lost to himself at any rate, and presently enquired,

" What day, and what day of the month

is it? I have not the slightest idea. I declare, it seems as if I had gone back to a little child — no more sense, knowledge or strength."

"It's Tuesday, and the eighteenth of August," said Ray; "don't you hear the locusts whir? — and the grass is full of those rustling, clicking insects that I'm not insectologer enough to give a name to."

Gilbert looked puzzled and incredulous. "The eighteenth of August!" he exclaimed.

"Yes," said Ray.

"And the last I remember it was the twenty-fifth of July! — I'd like to know where I've been for three weeks?"

"Not a great ways from this bed I should say," Ray answered, smiling; "but we've all kept track of time for you, so don't go to worrying. If you worry, or get excited, the doctor'll lay it all to me, and banish me to the school-room. He said he would; and he's a horrible man to keep his word."

"And this is my last summer!" said Gilbert, with a sigh, thinking how it had been broken up.

"Now, you dear old goose, what's the use of thinking of that?" said Ray, quickly. "It came pretty near being your last summer in earnest, and the rest of us are too glad to know it wasn't, to bother about books or study. Why, you're worth all the books in creation, and we'd a thousand times rather you'd be alive and not quite so smart, than to have you very wise and dead entirely."

"Softly, softly, Ray," said Mr. Winterhalter, who had put his head into the door in time to hear the conclusion of this speech. "Gilbert may be too weak to bear such a strong statement."

"Well, I don't know," said Gilbert, cheerily; "I don't feel exactly overwhelmed, yet. But it's better than medicine to hear him talk, I think."

Mr. Winterhalter must have thought so, or he would not have gone away and left them together.

"But," said Ray, as soon as the door shut, "you're no further behind, in studies, than the rest of us. We're all alike, for that matter; so don't you think anything more about it."

Gilbert lay silent for a long time after that, getting rested; and when he spoke it was to say, "When will school open?"

"There's no telling. It will all depend on you. I heard Mr. Winterhalter say he won't have the noise or confusion till you can bear it."

"Oh, but they're too good!" said Gilbert, quickly, with a suspicion of moisture in his eyes.

"No!" asserted Ray, stoutly, "they're not a bit too good! They're only grateful, —just as they ought to be. Mr. Winterhalter says, 'Gilbert risked his life for all of us; now he shall have everything for his comfort, and we'll wait till winter for him to get well, if it's necessary.' That's just what he said! and when 1 heard him say it I could have hugged him."

"Well," said Gilbert, "I'm not sure but they'll have to wait till winter for me. I'm just like a baby. Oh, but I can hardly stir my feet!" he added, making the attempt.

"I know," said Ray, with a great variety of expressions upon his face, the principal one being that of pity and sorrow,— Gilbert had been *so* strong and lithe and agile. "But what of it?" he asked, brightly; "you're as snug as can be, now, with nothing to do but to grow strong; and there isn't a fellow in school but what would carry you on his back if it was necessary."

Gilbert looked up, enquiringly. Ray looked down, happy and smiling. "It's true!" said he, "and you needn't look so amazed. Things have taken a turn or two since you were around, I can tell you."

Gilbert's eyes, which, since his illness, Ray declared had "grown bigger'n a cat's," said — as plainly as any words could have done — "Don't keep me waiting, but tell me all about it."

"Just as if you didn't know!—just as if you couldn't guess!" said Ray, delightedly. "Why, what *could* happen, but just what *has* happened? Do you suppose they haven't found out who was in our room during the sickness? and do you suppose they aren't grateful? Well, I should say *not* by the way they've trotted up to this door for the past week — first one, and then another, and then the whole of 'em together — asking, 'Is the captain better?' or, 'Is the captain looking lively this morning?' or, 'How *is* he, anyway, and does he say a word about us?'

Why, you dear old fellow, I've had my hands full with 'em!"

"And they called me captain?" said Gilbert, wonderingly.

"To be sure!—that's your rank."

"And it's all right?—they're all kind toward me, and just as they were once?"

"Yes; only your men never'll desert you again."

Gilbert's face grew very calm and peaceful. "I'm glad!" he said, drawing a long breath. Ray never knew, till then, how much the captain had felt the loss of his friends and his men.

"Why," he exclaimed, half-ready to cry at the look that was on Gilbert's face, "I didn't know that you felt so about. it. I thought you didn't mind, much. You're *so* funny, old fellow!—I never know how to take you. But it's all past, now," said Ray, softly; "it's all past, and there isn't a fellow

in the class but would go to the ends of the
earth for you, if it would do you any good."

Gilbert lay still a long time, — his grave,
wasted face looking very happy, — Ray
thought; then he opened his eyes, saying,
" But Gates ! Is he kind toward me, too ? "

Ray's face grew suddenly sober. He hesitated, stammered, tried to think of something else, and at last said nothing better
than, " Poor Gates ! "

But there was something in his tone and
grave face that told the whole story. Gilbert shivered a little, lay very still, thinking
of it, and finally asked, " When did he die ? "

" There ! you oughtn't to think of it ! "
said Ray, brightening up. " Mr. Winterhalter said I was to say nothing about it, — and
Gilbert, dear, *do* try to go to sleep or think
of something else, won't you ? "

But Gilbert said, " I can bear it, — I'm
strong enough ; and I 'd like to know."

" I oughtn't to tell you ! — but you are so
hard to deny. Well, it was one evening —
when you were the lowest — that — Oh, it
was the very evening, now I think of it, that
Forrest came over and offered to watch with
you, and Mrs. Winterhalter wouldn't let him,
because she hadn't dare trust you out of her
own hands. Well, it was that evening that
the doctor stayed here a great while, and
Mr. Winterhalter and Gates's mother — who
had come on — were both up there. It was
very still all over the house — it couldn't be
otherwise, you know, seeing that we were
only just able to be around — and we were
just going to bed in the school-room, when
Mr. Winterhalter came in and said that Gates
was dead. It was pretty sudden to us, and
the fellows were sober enough in a minute;
and before he went out, Mr. Winterhalter
said you were but just alive and we must
be as still as possible. There wasn't a

breath of noise after that, I can tell you!
The fellows all knew who had taken care
of them, and when they thought how they
had treated you — Well, there wasn't any
laughing and joking for a day or two. I'm
pretty certain that Tom Fowler cried a little,
though of course he would deny the fact.
But, oh dear!" cried Ray, bethinking himself, " I've tired you out, you poor old fellow! You look fagged and sleepy. I'll go
off this minute, and then you'll go to sleep."

And off he went, in spite of his friend's
protestations to the contrary. Gilbert did
not go to sleep. He lay thinking of his old
enemy; thinking and whispering gratefully,
" I'm glad I didn't treat him as I was tempted; I'm glad I didn't expose him to the
whole school! Now, no one beside Ray and
I need ever know what he did." Then some
happy tears came in his eyes at remember-

ing what Ray had said about his old friends,
and their regard for him, and he could only
say gratefully, " I am glad !   I am glad ! "

CHAPTER XV.

NOW that their old captain was once more able to talk and think, Mr. Winterhalter's boys began to grow impatient to see him. The room in which he lay had already grown to have a certain air of mystery about it, — the room in which Ray disappeared every morning, to come out only at noon and night, and where good Mrs. Winterhalter spent so much of her time, — and besides this, the time seems long and heavy-paced when one is waiting to look upon the long-hidden face of a friend, to hear the pleasant sound of his voice, and to feel the clasp of his hand which has almost been frozen in death.

So these impatient friends of Gilbert's, beset Mr. Winterhalter, one morning, pleading to be let in, if only for a minute, to "get a look at the poor old captain."

Mr. Winterhalter was kind and pleasant, but said, "No ; I must refuse for a few days longer. If I gave you permission now, I should be obliged to spoil all the pleasure by forbidding you to speak to him. Wait till he's a little stronger, and then you may go in and talk as much as you like."

"But Ray goes in every day," said they, "and talks as much as he likes."

"Ah," said the principal, "but that is a different matter. Can you not perceive that? But have patience and you shall go soon."

With this promise they had to be content, but as the days passed they fancied Mr. Winterhalter had forgotten all about his promise, and grew impatient again.

"I declare," Tom said, at dinner, one noon, "I don't think we're treated fairly, do you, boys? Here Mr. Winterhalter promised we might see the captain in a few days, and that was at least a week ago day before yesterday. I'd like to know what 'few' means in his dictionary?"

"Any indefinite period, probably," said Al Turner.

"It meant just twenty in old Banger's dictionary, down at Roncastle," said Barry White. "When he was going to punish us he used to shout, 'Come out here, sir, till I give you a few!'— then he always laid on just twenty with his rosewood ferule."

"Well," said Tom, "I could stand that better than suspense. I'd rather know that a few was just twenty, than to be guessing it was six or eight or a dozen, or any indefinite period, as Al says. Anyhow, I believe Mr. Winterhalter has forgotten, and the next

time I see him I shall bid him — gently, but
firmly, as the story-books say — to recollect
himself. You needn't smile, Ray Hunter! —
of course you've got the advantage of us,
and of course you know it. I don't blame
you, but I'd like to be in your boots, anyhow."

"You needn't," said Ray, contentedly,
"and there's no need of giving Mr. Winterhalter a reminder. He told me that you
were all to see Gilbert this afternoon. I
thought I wouldn't tell you before dinner
for fear of impairing your appetites —
they're *so* very poor, already."

The boys, like all convalescents, *were*
slightly voracious.

"Is that so?" said Tom, dropping knife
and fork; "and we're really to see him this
afternoon? Well!"

This "Well!" of Tom's expressed a good
deal, and conversation dwindled away to

nothing. Now that the long-looked for time
had come, they were thinking, with much
inward trepidation, what they should say
when they stood face to face with the friend
they had injured. The bare thought made
Tom very nervous all the rest of dinner-
time ; and when the meal was over and the
rest were hurrying away in preparation to
"see the captain," he followed Ray and
stopped him in the hall.

" Look here," Tom said, getting Ray by
the button-hole of his blouse, and looking
very awkward and uncomfortable ; " what on
earth can I say to the captain when I see
him ? There won't be an idea in my head —
I•know there won't ! And I'd like to —
to — to say something about the way I've
treated him, you know, and ask him to forgive me. But when I once put eyes on him,
I shall stand there like a great wooden block-
head, without an idea in my whole frame

and no hopes of getting one if I was to be hung for it. Now, what can I say?"

" Say?" said Ray, laughing a bit, in spite of himself, " why, say just what comes into your head,—just what you feel! That's all I can tell you, so let me go."

" Well," said Tom, in evident despair, " I shall make a dreadful muss of it, somehow. I know I shall!"

" But you needn't!" laughed Ray. " Say just what you feel — no matter how it sounds — and then it will all be right."

It was a little after two, when Ray heard a soft and rather hesitating rap at the study-door. " They 've come," he said, under his breath, to Gilbert, and went to the door — looking back to nod and laugh at the timorous summons.

Mrs. Winterhalter had come in with her great work-basket and was sitting beside Gilbert, but finding that the boys were without, she rose at once, knowing — kind heart — that her presence would be something of a restraint, upon the free expressions of their feelings. As she passed out the boys came hesitatingly in.

The room was a little dim, and at first their eyes were unused to the subdued light, but presently they perceived the captain, and actually sitting up! It was the first time, and Ray had put the big chair by one of the windows, and for half-an-hour had busied himself about his friend in preparation for this expected reception. Now, as the boys caught sight of their old captain among his pillows and cushions — looking the very shadow of the strong, healthy Gilbert Starr they had last seen — they stopped in the middle of the room with faces full of awe, and hearts very soft and tender, for such great sturdy fellows as they. Silently they stood there — as if afraid that

the sound of their voices would dispel the
vision in the arm-chair — and looked at Gilbert and each other, and then at Ray, till at
last it was getting to be very awkward and
embarrassing.

Then Ray said, with that merry ring in
his tone which none of the others had,

"Come, you group of statuary!—you
matchless tableau!—it's only Gilbert!"

Fortunately, this broke the spell, and Tom
remembered what he had come for. Hastily
stepping forward and regarding Gilbert with
a mixture of expressions that any other time
would have been laughable enough, he came
up to his old captain's chair and shyly held
out his hand. In an instant Gilbert's own
white, wan one lay within it.

Tom looked down at it, lying so weak and
helpless in his own great brown hand,
hought of all that had passed, and began
to choke and shake. Knowing what was

coming and striving vainly to avert it, and
feeling, as he afterwards expressed it—"like
a confounded great baby that had lost its
mother"—he suddenly gave away, and
hurriedly sitting down on the hassock by
Gilbert's feet, hid his face in one of the
cushions. Here he shook from head to foot,
though all his sobs were smothered by the
friendly pillows.

I think this did more toward putting them
on their old level of happy friendship than
any words or pleadings for forgiveness could
have done. Tom's warm, hearty, honest
grief for past misdeeds, spoke for them all.
He had, though unintentionally, told Gilbert
just what he felt, as Ray advised; and Ray,
looking on, felt that Tom had done the best
thing that could have been done toward
restoring the broken, long trampled-upon
friendship.

Gilbert's gray eyes got very dim and

misty, and grew mistier still as one by one his old men came forward to take his hand. They looked at him with awe in their faces, wondering all the time why he had brought himself into the very grasp of death for their sake, and feeling half-surprised, some of them, that there was no hint of this high courage and sacrifice in his face,— that it had not changed into the face of a martyr, or an ideal hero, or something grand to look upon, since the ordeal through which he had passed.

But the same old Gilbert it was, save the thinness, and as he looked up at them through the dimness of his kind eyes, saying, " It's pleasant to look at you again, Barry," or, " I'm glad to see you once more, Albert," they felt, somehow, as if all the time they had had a prince in disguise among them, and that now he had showed his royalty they could not be too faithful to him, too grateful, nor too proud of the heroism that made him royal.

Some of them stooped to whisper in Gilbert's ear,— words that their hearts had long been aching to breathe to him. But Tom still kept his face hidden — of what are boys more ashamed than their tears? — though his sobbing was ⬤er. The rest of the boys, through with their hand-shaking and congratulations, had settled themselves around Gilbert on the chairs, hassocks, or whatever afforded a seat; but there sat Tom, immovable as a statue. But suddenly, in the midst of their talk, he made a desperate effort and raised his head, hastily dashed away his tears, and slowly met Gilbert's eyes. Gilbert never looked brighter or kinder than at that moment, Ray thought, and poor Tom remembered with a pang the look his face had worn on that long-ago Sunday afternoon.

" Well, Tom," said Gilbert, " I 've told the others how glad I am to see them. Now may I tell you ? "

Tom had yet such a choking in his throat, and was so afraid of breaking down entirely, that he just took Gilbert's thin hand — pressing it between both of his — and said nothing.

" I suspect that I 've got you to thank," continued Gilbert, gratefully, " for doing me a great favor a long time ago. Haven't I ? "

" Favors ! " groaned Tom ; " don't talk to me about favors unless you want to kill me entirely."

" But I can thank you for this," said Gilbert. " It was a great favor. I should have lost my head-boy's rank but for it, and I thank you very much."

Tom's eyes opened very wide. " I — I — I don't know what you mean," he stammered ; " there's a mistake somewhere, for I haven't done you a favor in more than one term."

Gilbert's turn came to look surprised. "Why, you must have forgotten," he said, looking at Tom; "I mean the packet of papers which you returned to me — hid in my bed — just in time to save me from losing my rank."

The blank look of astonishment on Tom's face at once showed Gilbert that he had made a mistake. He looked at Ray in surprise, then dropped his eyes upon the coverlet, feeling that if he looked around at the faces of his companions he should discover something which it was much better to leave undiscovered; but Ray, who sat a little in the shadow of his friend's chair, saw that Albert Turner's face flushed crimson. Nothing more was said about the matter then.

They spent the time very happily till the

study-clock struck four, and then Mr. Winterhalter came in and said that, considering the manner in which Gilbert's eyes drooped and cheeks flushed, it was desirable that their visit should draw to a close.

They were a good many minutes in taking leave, and Ray went away with them to give his friend an opportunity to go to sleep. Hardly had Gilbert closed his eyes, when somebody brushed lightly past his chair and laid a hand upon his shoulder. Supposing it to be Mrs. Winterhalter, he was greatly surprised on looking up, to find Albert Turner standing there.

"I knew you would be surprised," said Gilbert's old secretary, "but I couldn't tell you before the rest. It was I who returned your papers."

"You!" said Gilbert.

"Yes; and I helped rob you." Gilbert looked incredulous. "Oh, but it's true!"

said Turner, turning his eyes away. "I did it to rob you. I meant to do it. I haven't any excuse." What could Gilbert say to this? "But when I saw what a fellow it would be the means of putting in your place, I couldn't have anything to do with it any longer. I—I hated him for getting me into the plot. But he's dead, now, and—and I wish, sometimes, I was dead with him."

Then Gilbert spoke.

"Why do you wish so?" he asked.

Albert made no reply, and kept his face averted. Gilbert knew that he wanted to crave forgiveness, and that either a high pride or emotion kept him silent; and at last Albert's old captain said, "It's a dreadful thing for a fellow to carry about such a load with him, feeling every moment weighed down with shame and meanness. I know what it is, Al."

" You ! " said Turner ; " how can you ? "

" It was about Mr. Winterhalter's flag.
You remember how we won that unfairly ?
Well, it stung me week after week, just
as I think this stings you."

Albert's proud face drooped on his shoulder a little.   This evil *had* stung him.   Now
it seemed quite unfortunate that Mr. Winterhalter should come in at that moment, looking slightly displeased at finding Turner
there, and that he should be obliged to go
away without another word upon the subject.   But the next time Gilbert saw him,
he came into the study holding out his hand.

" Will you forgive me ? " he said at once.
There is no need of writing Gilbert's answer.   " I ought to have asked you before,"
Albert said, " when I had that good chance ;
but it stuck in my throat, somehow, and I
couldn't say it.   I don't expect you 'll trust
me as you did before, but you 're not to
blame for that."

To which Gilbert answered, "Only wait and see, before you decide."

Some quiet, pleasant days followed this, in which Gilbert gained strength and activity very fast. They had him in the garden soon, rolling him up and down the gravel-walks in the big study-chair, and from that he went to using his feet in short walks along the paths, leaning on Ray's shoulder the while.

Preparations were going forward for the re-opening of school, and already the old, long-absent pupils began to return; and on the last evening that was left of this long, sad vacation, Gilbert and Ray were slowly pacing down the long central walk of the garden which led them at last out to a wide terrace full of shrubbery, and with a lookout upon the far-stretching picture that hill and valley made. The sun had just hidden its splendid face behind Riverside, but afar on hill and mountain-top its light quivered and gleamed — loth to leave the happy earth. Far and smooth stretched the beryl-tinted meadows to the foot of the soft gray hill-barrier, through which the winding river cut its path to the sea, and wherever the eye turned, all the land smiled warm and peaceful and golden up to the summer sky.

As Ray and Gilbert came out to this look-out upon an enchanted land, voices met them, and presently Gilbert saw Tom and the remainder of the Boat Club coming up the terrace-walk, and what seemed very strange, they were all in their scarlet jackets as if bound for a boat-race. Then he suddenly noted that Ray had on his uniform, too.

Ray paused, according to a concerted plan, doubtless, and the Club came up. Tom stepped out from their midst, and suddenly caught Gilbert as if he intended

to carry out a premeditated assault, and
what was stranger still, Ray' offered no
resistance, but stood looking on very contentedly.

Then Tom said, in his hearty, blunt
manner, "We don't mean that gold, or any
thing like it, can show what we feel toward
you, but we'd just like you to wear this,
if you will, — partly to show our liking,
and partly to tell you that we want to make
you our captain again, — that is, if you'll
consent to command such a set of fellows.
Say, will you ? "

This conclusion was not quite according
to the programme, but it answered very
well, and served to show what was upper-
most in Tom's mind; and as he stepped
back there shone on Gilbert's breast a
golden C, cunningly twisted through a pair
of tiny oars, — "to show our liking," and the
badge of his restored rank. What do you

suppose was Gilbert's answer? Then they moved slowly back to the house, very happy indeed, and not very quiet about it.

CHAPTER XVI.

SCHOOL was reopened on the first day of
the first autumn month, — not for a new
term, but to finish the one whose best days
had been so sadly marred by the fever.
Once more familiar faces were to be seen
everywhere, with here and there a new one.
The lawn, at play-time, was covered with
boys whose shouts and merry-making were
not unpleasant to hear, after the silence and
loneliness that had clung so long about
the great school-buildings and the pleasant
grounds. The halls echoed, the stairs were
noisy with climbing feet, and in garden,
school-room, and the long eating-hall, there

275

was the pleasant stir of life again,— a pleasant, happy life they thought it.

Studies were taken up where the fever
had broken them off, and though no one
hoped to pass such a successful examination as might have been passed but for the
interruption in the middle of the term, yet
most of Mr. Winterhalter's boys went to
work in a quiet, persevering way that was
quite satisfactory to the head of the school.
But this interruption of studies, that had
"taken a great slice out of the summer,"
as Tom Fowler said, interfered more seriously with the plans of the First Class. They
were to graduate at the end of the term,
and of course wished to do so with honor;
but with that great gap to bridge over in
one short month,— well, the prospect of
a brilliant examination was not remarkably
bright. But as this was nothing for which
they were in fault, they settled down to

books and hard work, bound to do as well as possible, and let the brilliancy take care of itself.

Gilbert took up his books once more, and felt as one feels to get among long-absent friends; and now, as day after day passed, he began to think of the near-approach of the last day of the term, — the last day he was to spend in the dear, pleasant building which had grown to be home to him. No other place, he thought, could ever be like Rainford to him; no friends like the Winterhalters; no other spot in the wide earth such a home.

The great building had sheltered him since he was a little eleven-year-old boy. It was the only real home he had ever known, and every nook and corner were as dear and familiar to him as the home-haunts of other boys are to them. The Winterhalters were like kind parents. Do you wonder, then, that he looked forward to the time of leaving Rainford and these friends with regret?

Ray and he were talking the matter over, and Gilbert said, with a shadow on his face, "This place has got to be home to me,— I didn't know how much of a home till I began to think of going. Just think, I've been here since I was ten — eleven years old, and now I am a long way past seventeen; and I haven't spent a vacation away from Rainford in the whole time, except the one I took with you. Do you wonder that it's like pulling up one's tent to pitch — well, that's the question — where?"

" Why, you 'll go to college, of course," said Ray; "that's decided already; and all you 've got to do is to decide which it shall be."

" Well, that's not the easiest matter in the world," said Gilbert.

"Of course not; but then, you needn't be very particular. You'll get LL. D. and Dr. Phil. tacked on to your name before we know it."

" I 've been here a long, long time," said Gilbert, musingly, "and the fellows that were in the First Class, when I came and was way down in the Fourth, are twenty-five or six, now, and got boys of their own."

" Well," said Ray, " don't go to scraping in the 'ashes of the ancient past,' — not just yet. Wait a bit, and let's talk about the college. Now Rainford isn't half as much to me as to you, and I'd rather, on the whole, be in a university than here. I only wish I was sure, as you are, that I could enter." ·

" Aren't you?" said Gilbert.

" No; father hasn't said a word to me about it, yet. But then, there's no telling anything by that. He won't speak till the last minute, and when he does he'll think twenty minutes are as good as a month to decide in."

"But your mother?"

"Oh, she wants me to go, I think; and go I shall if she says the word, because she won't speak till she's sure of what father thinks. And if she *does* once speak, it will be to have me go where you do!" Ray added, jubilantly.

"Sure?" smiled Gilbert.

"Yes! that is all certain, if some other things aren't. Mother will send me off under your wing, confident that I shall come out straight without fail. So I shall!" Ray exclaimed, dropping his book, and whirling about on one boot-heel with a chair spinning on one leg for an accompaniment.

"Are any of the other fellows in our class going?" Gilbert asked.

"I don't know; they don't, I believe.

Turner hasn't decided, and Tom — well, to tell the truth, the great honest fellow doesn't care enough for books to go any further. He says he's dumb-founded to think that he's actually going to graduate this term."

Gilbert laughed a little, took up his books, and began studying; and so the question was no nearer a decision than it had been a dozen times before. But an evening or two after this, the important question of where the tent should be pitched came near being finally decided.

Ray bounced into the Club chamber, where nearly all the class were studying their lessons, with a packet of letters from the mail-bag which had just been opened in the hall below.

" A letter for each one of us, except Bob Upham," he cried out, tossing the buff and white enveloped missives to their respective owners; "and here's two for you, and one for me, Gilbert," he added, as he came to their table. "That's about your proportion of every good thing, — just double the quantity of mine."

"This is from my guardian, Mr. Steuben, — I know his handwriting," Gilbert said, taking up one of the letters. "He always writes me one letter a term, never any more, never any less; and then feels that he has done his duty, I suppose."

Then he tore open the envelope, while Ray looked on, saying, "I wonder if there's anything about leaving Mr. Winterhalter's, in it?"

This was what he found in Mr. Steuben's big round handwriting, and read aloud to Ray, — both putting their heads together over the study-table:

"SOUTHFIELD, SEP. 15.

To GILBERT STARR :

I have a rather indistinct recollection of

receiving a letter from you some time last spring, informing me that this was to be your last term at Mr. Winterhalter's — " " There ! " said Ray, in a whisper, " it's coming ! " — " or in other words that you were to graduate this fall. This being the case, I suppose it is best that you should begin to consider what school or college you are next to enter. If you are prepared to enter college at once, you have only to decide which of the many in the land you prefer, as I have no choice for you. If you are *not* yet ready, there is a good opportunity to enter the school at Framwick, where you could probably soon fit yourself to enter a university. I hope you will make the decision ere long, and communicate the same to me. I enclose a check, payable to your order, which I think will cover all your expenses at Mr. Winterhalter's. If not, you must inform me.

Perhaps, in view of the fact that it is now nearly seven years since you entered school, and have not, during that period, spent a vacation in Southfield, you would like to spend the coming one with us.

Respectfully,

N. P. STEUBEN."

"What a man!" said Ray, indignantly, as the letter was folded up; "he don't give you an invitation to come and see him, but says *perhaps* you'd like to. Of course you'll do no such thing!"

"I don't know," said Gilbert, gravely; "I'd like to see Southfield once more, and Mr. Steuben — a little."

"Now!" cried Ray, getting out of his chair with indignation, "now, you Gilbert Starr! That's a pretty way to be changing the programme — at this late day, when I'd got my mind made up to take you home with me, when mother and father will expect you, and when you *know* it's the very thing I 've been looking forward to for a whole year. Now if you 'll go to serving me like that, and go off to that ●l, out-of-the-way Southfield to spend vacation with an unheard of Mr. Steuben that don't care a copper for you — I 'll — I 'll — "

"You 'll what?" said Gilbert; "there must be some dreadful penalty on the end of that long supposition."

"Well, I shall think hard of you," said Ray, trying to look his grimest.

Gilbert tore open his second letter, and while lost in surprise at what he found therein, Ray, who had been hastily skimming over the contents of his own home-letter, thrust the missive under his eyes, exclaiming triumphantly, "It's just as I said. Read what mother says." And so perforce, Gilbert was obliged to read : " Tell Gilbert that under no consideration must he think of spending his vacation elsewhere than with you and with us. We shall expect him, and feel disappointed if he does not come."

"There," said Ray, eloquently, "will you disappoint her?"

"No — perhaps — really, Ray, I'm thinking of something else, or trying to. I've got a letter from — from — Well, I doubt my very eyes!"

"Private?" asked Ray.

"Not to you," said Gilbert. Then they both read together:

> *Room* 9, *at* 57 *Eustace Place*,
> *Sept.* 16, 18 —.

My Dear Starr:

I hope you have not forgotten those little hints which I dropped upon examination-day at Mr. Winterhalter's. I told that good gentlemen, at the time, that we wanted you at our college, and informed him, in a roundabout way, that he must use his influence in our behalf; but, fearing he has not done so, I send you this little note as a reminder of what was said at that time. I think he told me that you had no parents living, and would probably be free to make your own choice of universities. If this is the case, do not decide without considering the claims which our ancient, elm-shadowed institution presents to all who wish a solid, thorough education. Do not imagine that I am begging for the college, — we are already full to overflowing, — for it is *you* that I wish to benefit. I want you here, will give you a good welcome, and hope I may have that pleasure soon.

Yours truly,

CHARLES BAINSLEY."

"Professor Bainsley!" cried Ray, as he came to the conclusion. Then he sat down and stared at his friend with a very blank face.

" Well ? " said Gilbert, after he had re turned Ray's stare for about five minutes.

" Yale ! and a letter from a professor ! " gasped Ray.

" Yes."

" And you're not astonished ? — not gone ' clean daft,' as the Scotch say ? "

" Well, I *am* astonished ! " said Gilbert; and his face showed it.

" Astonished ! — that doesn't express *my* sensations. I feel as Tom Fowler did when he got to sleep in service, and woke up to find the lamps out and himself locked in — ' *dreadful* tumbled up, you know, somehow.' But," added Ray — his face beginning to shine with delight at his friend's good fortune — " you deserve it, and I 'm glad for you, old fellow."

" What in the world are you two talking

so much about?" said Turner, from his study-table; "I should think you'd never finish your letters."

"I know!" said Ray; "Gilbert's such a bother — interrupts me — sticks his letter into my face — looks over my shoulder — gets my news, and don't give me a minute's peace. I bear with him, though."

Then they put their letters away and took up their books but Ray was so excited and jubilant over the professor's letter, that studying was not an easy matter. He wanted to hit Gilbert's elbow continually, and ask him if this letter had not decided the question of colleges entirely; but as Gilbert was deep in his books, forbore. Several days more of the fast-flitting month passed, and though Gilbert put off answering both his guardian's and Professor Bainsley's letter, wanting time to think of it, as he said, yet Ray was confident that, in his own mind, Gilbert had decided for the elm-shadowed college. Just here something occurred to change the subject of discussion, and for a few days colleges and professors were little thought about.

Tom Fowler came up the lawn one twilight, just back from a walk to Rainford, where he had met Forrest of the Riverside school.

"You're just the two fellows I want see," said he, his brown face lit up with enthusiasm, as he came on the piazza where Gilbert and Al Turner stood. "What do you think is up? Why, I met Forrest up in town and he wanted me to ask you to race, — race with the two dear old boats that we have hardly stepped into this summer. Wouldn't you like it, Captain? — wouldn't you, Al? We've all got to leave pretty quick, you know, and then the boats pass into the fellows' hands that take our places.

Who knows we 'll ever have a chance to handle an oar again, or feel the old river swelling under us?" Tom added, with a strong sensation of choking in his throat. Turner was silent, waiting for Gilbert to speak.

CHAPTER XVII.

DID THE SUMMER TEACH ANYTHING?

WELL," said Gilbert, "it *would* be pleasant. I'd like to race above all things; but isn't the 'Triton' laid up?"

"No! and you may thank me for that!" said Tom, eagerly. "I went down to the boat-house the other day, and there was the poor old thing dry as a cork; and thinking I'd have one more float before I went—just for the sake of old times—I put it afloat to be ready for some Saturday. So we're in luck! for when I came along, just now, I stopped to look, and the 'Triton' was as sound and snug as a nut."

" If that is so," said Gilbert, " we 'll race. I 'd like to very much. Wouldn't you, Al ? "

" Yes — after practise," said the secretary.

" Of course we shall practise," put in Tom; " we haven't handled an oar in so long."

Ray joined them just then. " What's up ? " said he.

" A race !" said Tom; " a genuine, old-fashioned race, with Gilbert for captain and Forrest for a rival. Doesn't that seem natural ? "

" Yes, that's good ! And when is it to be ? "

" That's what we haven't talked about," said Gilbert. " What did Forrest say, Tom ? "

" Oh, he wasn't particular; any time toward the last few days we're to be here. Only, when you've decided, he'd like to know."

"Yes; and Al shall write a note," said Gilbert.

Then, after a little more talk about the day which would be best for the race, they answered the bell's call and went in to supper.

The coming event seemed to revive all their old fondness for boating. What time could possibly be spared from books — it was not a great deal — they spent in the 'Triton' on the river, and there was much need of the practise if they had any intention of being the victors. Such a long time it had been since they had pulled together, that muscles were found to have grown surprisingly weak, and arms and backs had a way of aching that astonished their possessors.

"I don't know what we'll do," Tom sighed, "when we get where there's no river and no boat. I expect that we shall grow into a parcel of weak-backed, small-muscled fellows, anyhow."

This boat practise, and their books, kept them busy enough, and made the days seem very short. Altogether too fast, they thought, the days hurried on to examination week, and the time when they were to leave Rainford, the boats, the river, and their books forever.

Mr. Winterhalter called Gilbert into the study one morning, to ask him when the proposed race was to come off.

"The afternoon of examination-day," said Gilbert, — "after we're through with the exercises."

"Will not the day after do as well?" asked the principal.

"Hardly," the captain answered, "because most of us start for home. But if you object — "

"No, no, Gilbert, I don't object to the

race," said Mr. Winterhalter, quickly; "it's having so much done on examination-day that I don't like. I am afraid that either the exercises will crowd upon the time set for the race, or *vice versa.* Now what would you say to taking the afternoon before?"

"But our lessons!—we're in the school-room, you know, at that time," said Gilbert.

"Not if I excuse you," said Mr. Winter-halter, "as I think I had better."

"We shall like the plan, of course," said Gilbert, smiling; "but you—"

"Well," interrupted Mr. Winterhalter, with something like a sigh, "I can afford to be lenient, I think, seeing that I am not to have another oppotrunity to do you a favor. You can have next Thursday afternoon."

Gilbert thanked him, and went away to tell the good news and send a message to Forrest announcing the change of time.

Thursday morning, to everybody's disappointment, dawned gray and moist with rain, and there were some anxious faces on both sides the river; but toward noon, to their delight and surprise, the heavy clouds drifted off into the south-east, and the sun came out broad, full and hearty. At noon, as the Boat Club left their lessons and went to put on their uniforms, you would never suspected the day to have brought mist and shower at its dawning.

Now, though this may not be pleasant to you who remember the crowd and the excitement that attended last summer's races between the two schools, this race was to be private, in a measure, as no one outside of, and but few within the schools, knew that it was to take place.

Forrest and Gilbert were now too strong friends to be the bitter rivals that they had been on the previous summer, and, as Forrest said, "We're just having this for our own comfort, without any crowd or speeches or bother to it." Forrest had a friend — "as honorable as can be " — he declared to Gilbert, who would act as judge, and to this proposition Captain Starr assented, with a faith in his rival's integrity that was pleasant to see.

As Gilbert and his men went down the lawn to the boat-house about two o'clock, they saw that Forrest and his crew were already at their place upon the river.

"Their time, on the other side of the river, must be faster than ours," said Gilbert, looking at his watch, "for it's only two, and we were not to start till ten minutes past. However, we'll push off."

Forrest's men gave them a salute as they came alongside, and Forrest said to Gilbert, "Do your best and beat us, my dear fellow ! We'll take anything from you, this afternoon — except a tip-over. This is my friend,

Walter Kenyon, in the judge's boat. Kenyon, this is Captain Starr." The two shook hands over their boat's side; and then, at the word, the rival boats started down stream.

No sunnier day had the year seen — none more pure or cloudless. A faint breeze fluttered seaward. Gilbert, in the midst of his watchful seconds, remembered two other days like this — only in the middle of summer — when a little figure sat watching him from shore, — a little figure that now slumbered up in the quiet brow of Riverside, unconscious of the busy hum below, the river's merry ripple, and the down.gliding of the happy-heated racers.

He had to put this remembrance away as speedily as possible, and turn his face resolutely toward the point for which they were making, down where the river flashed into dazzling radiance like a mirror turned in the sunlight.

They had got more than half-way down, with no perceptible advantage on the side of either boat, when suddenly Forrest cried out, " Stop ! we 're crippled ! "

Gilbert looked, saw Forrest and his men making vain snatches at an oar that was dancing lightly away on the ripples, while their boat swung half-around, and gave word for his crew to stop. When they did come to a standstill the " Triton " was many lengths ahead of its rival.

" Now here's a pretty go ! " said Tom, with an impatient face, as he rested on his oars.

" Turn, and go back," said Gilbert, quickly; and presently they were alongside the " Mermaid."

Forrest was biting his lips and trying to hold his temper, and as they came up said not a word.

" Well," said Gilbert, not without some vexation in his tone, " this is unfortunate ! "

"I don't see how it happened!" said the fellow who had lost his oar; "the first I knew it was adrift and out of my reach."

Forrest looked as if he thought this a most miserable excuse and wished to say so. For a minute there was silence — save the musical gurgle of water round the prow of the "Triton" — while disappointment and vexation settled upon all faces. The long-looked for race to end like this! — all their afternoon's pleasure to be spoiled by such a foolish, awkward mishap!

Then Gilbert, seeing how matters were going to go, said, "Of course you won't think of racing now, — with one oar gone."

"No," said Forrest, gloomily.

"Well, seeing that we can't help ourselves, let's keep on down to the Island, land, and finish the day there. Then we'll not lose our boating — it's quite a pull down there, you know — and we all want to visit the

Island before we go. And we may have a first-rate time, after all," added Gilbert, brightly.

Forrest looked up gratefully, but not more gratefully than the fellow who had been so unfortunate as to lose his oar, and who felt as if all his companions regarded him as the cause of their disappointment.

"Well," said the captain of the Riverside school, "I agree to that. No one but you, Starr, would have thought of mending up the trip in this style. Now, if I can only make Walter understand, and have him come down, too, we'll go on first-rate."

But Kenyon, who had seen this balk in the race, was already coming down to them.

The Island was a long way down the river,— at least half-a-mile below the point where the race-boats turned to go back. It lay in the middle of the river, just where the stream began to narrow and sweep through the hills, and was low and flat, with a great hickory towering out of its center.

The boys caught sight of the old tree's yellow blaze of foliage after a long, sturdy pull, and Tom said, "If all the nuts aren't picked up, maybe we'll call it as good as a race, captain;— though I *did* want to whip Forrest and his men before leaving Rainford for good. But if we can have a hickory-crack!— well, it won't be the worst thing that could have happened."

"Oh, we'll have a good time, yet," said Gilbert, cheerily.

"It's an ill wind that blows no good," said Barry White, "and we shouldn't have seen the Island again, but for this."

And, making the best of their misfortune, they came down, at last, to their destination, ran the "Triton's" prow in among the rank river-grass, and landed. The "Mermaid" was a little way behind.

Tom's first care was to see whether the hickory-nuts were abundant. He came back, after his search, to where Gilbert and the rest were waiting for Forrest and his men, saying, "It's the first time that I ever knew hickory-nuts to be laying around in this style. There's a bushel out yonder if there's one, and just think!—only a little over a mile from Rainford town. What's going to happen, Gilbert Starr?—the millennium, or what?"

Forrest and Kenyon and the others landed, and soon the island was noisy enough with this gay and somewhat boisterous company which had taken possession of it. It would be difficult to tell all the ways in which they passed hour after hour away,—short, pleasant, blithesome hours, and every moment of them given up to full, hearty sport which, perhaps, was a little madder and wilder than usual, in view of the fact that it was their last frolic together.

They were great grown boys, but fun and frolic were not out of them yet, by any means. They raced and jumped, and climbed to the top of the hickory tree,— in getting down from, which, Tom Fowler tore his scarlet jacket half off him, but consoled himself with thinking that it was the last time he should wear it and it was no matter, —and at last began to sober down into the gravity that is expected of young gentlemen of their age. Then they fell to cracking hickory-nuts. They were scattered here and there in little groups, all about the island, laughing and joking over their nuts, and talking — some of them — very boisterously.

Gilbert sat near the water's edge — alone at first, for Ray and Kenyon were together — but soon Forrest sauntered that way, and after taking a look or two at Gilbert's face to see whether he was in a mood for company, seated himself beside him.

"It's been a jolly afternoon, hasn't it?"
said he, helping himself to his friend's pile
of nuts; "better than any racing I think,
for then we should have just rowed down
and back and gone home, and that would
have been the end of it. I think it was
fortunate that Wayne lost his oar, though I
was vexed enough at the time to 've thrown
him overboard. Starr," he exclaimed, with
sudden earnestness, "how on earth do you
hold your temper when you feel like knock-
ing a fellow down?"

"Why do you ask that?" said Gilbert,
smiling a little as he looked up.

"Well — I was thinking I felt just like
serving Wayne so when he lost his oar, and
I had to bite my teeth together and *push*
the feeling down. I suppose I'm what your
funny Tom Fowler would call a ' hard-bitted'
fellow : at any rate it doesn't come easy for
me to do a good and graceful thing."

--

"Does it to many?" said Gilbert.

"I don't know, — I thought it did; to you, for instance, Starr."

"Well," said Gilbert, after a space in which they both were busy, cracking nuts, "you've made a mistake. It's *not* easy for one to do a right thing, — it's very hard."

"Yet — well, I don't quite like to say it to your face, but it's the truth, and I've been wanting this chance a great while — you 're my good genius!"

"What?" said Gilbert, dropping the stone that served for a nut-cracker.

"There, don't forget yourself," said Forrest. "I only said the truth. You're my good genius — that's the only name I can think of, and that doesn't express just what I mean — and you've been to me for a whole year — well, I can't tell you how much! You see," Forrest continued, throwing a handful of nut-shells into the water and

watching them as they floated away on the
ripples, "I've watched you a long time
— you may be sure *you* weren't allowed to
know it!—and I've kept you under my eyes
pretty closely all summer, and the good
you've done me isn't to be told by any words
that I possess."

Gilbert looked puzzled.

"Aren't you just a little mistaken, Forrest?" said he.

"No! Having never been in my place,
you can't realize what I mean," said Forrest,
earnestly; "but this is the way it is. When
a fellow is all afloat, and knows that he isn't
what he should be, I tell you he looks about
for something to settle upon,—you know
that! Well, that was the case with me for a
long time. I knew I wasn't honorable, that
I shirked duty, that I was wrong all around,
and there wasn't a fellow in school that felt
as I did about it. So I looked over here to

you. Now, I don't claim but what I'd ought
to fought the question out myself, but
that isn't the way with a fellow, sometimes.
He wants to see somebody else in the same
fix with himself, and see how they come out
in the fight. So I watched you — and waited. You got on, and I took courage. The
Boat Club pulled you down from your rank
for being honest and saying your prayers,
and then I watched you with both of my
eyes. That was the crisis. If you had
yielded and gone under, it would all have
been over with me, too. You didn't know
how much depended on your actions, then,
and by the way, isn't that always the way
with such things?"

Gilbert made no reply. He had stopped
cracking nuts and was looking soberly at
the seaward-gliding tide.

"Well," continued Forrest, "you didn't
go under, and that saved me! You kept

on in the path you had chosen, and I began
to think of getting into the same way myself. Do you remember what I whispered
to you that night, when you had gone to
bed after getting into the ice ? "

"Yes; you said, 'Will you help me?'
But I haven't !" said Gilbert, regretfully.

"Yes, you have !" said Forrest,— "more
than I can ever thank you for. You've
helped me every day of your life ; you've
been my good genius. Do you understand
me now, Starr ? "

"Yes," said Gilbert.

"Now," said Forrest, throwing the stone
which he had used into the water, " we may
drift apart just as those ripples will drift
out of sight and be lost to view, but I didn't
want to part from you without letting you
know what you, unconsciously, had done for
me. I think the good will never quite leave
me whatever evil I get into; at any rate,"
he added, dropping his handsome face a

little, " I pray, in my prayers, that God will keep me; and it seems, sometimes, that I never can be grateful enough for what this summer has taught me."

" Why," said Gilbert, meeting Forrest's eyes with his own gray ones, " that is my thought, too ! Do you know, it has seemed to me that this summer, from its very beginning, through the fever and — and deaths, and all that has come upon us, has, every day of it, been a lesson. And now that we're just through with it, I look back and wonder at all it has taught — more than I can tell you, Forrest."

Afar upon the level river, upon the low meadows, upon the soft gray barrier of the hills the sun shot a last ray of pure golden light that touched them wondrously; and looking thither Forrest was silent, though his clear-cut, manly face was all aglow with the deep thoughts that stirred his soul.

Then Ray and Kenyon sauntered up,

arm-in-arm, Ray saying, "What fellows you are for hickory-nuts! The rest of us were through eating long ago, and Gilbert, do you know its sundown and growing chilly?"

Gilbert looked up. "So it is!" he said; "how the time has flown!"

"I should think so!" said Ray, scanning Gilbert's face; "you and Forrest haven't known, for the last half-hour, whether the river was flowing up or down, whether you were in boats or on the land."

Then Gilbert called men; and then came the bustle of getting under way amid much laughter and pleasant talk and plashing of oars.

"Shall I see you again?" Gilbert said to the captain of the "Mermaid," as the two boats were on the point of departure.

"Oh, to be sure!" said Forrest, as his crew pushed off; "I'll find time for a minute with you some time to-morrow. Good night, my dear fellow!"

And as the " Mermaid " went skimming over
the purpling water homeward, with its generous, manly captain waving back his farewell,
Gilbert looked upon him for the last time ;
for the next day he was detained and did
not keep his promise, and before two more
years had fled, the brave, bright life was
quenched under the sunny waters of a far-off
Indian sea. Gilbert thought, then, of what
the dear fellow had said about the summer's
teaching.

Now, it was so late when the "Triton "
and its crew reached home, that the Rainford
bells were ringing for evening services, and
as they stopped a minute on the wharf to
listen to their tender chiming, Gilbert said,
" Dear old bells ! — and the last time they
are to ring for me. O, Ray, what an afternoon this has been ! — crowded so full of
sober and thoughtful and yet pleasant
things ! "

CHAPTER XVIII.

FAREWELLS.

THE last day of the term was one of those matchless October days that crown the ripe year with a gentle splendor, — the gorgeous hills shining through a purple vestment, the river throbbing slowly seaward, cloud and sky and earth alike full of tender magnificence.

The examination exercises were neither lengthy nor very brilliant. They passed off well, and gave satisfaction to the not very large audience. There was a tacit understanding between parents and scholars that nothing sparkling or unusually brilliant

314

was to be expected; the great gap in the summer study had forbidden this.

The graduating class acquitted themselves well, and were looked upon as having fitted themselves thoroughly and soundly for the work that life was to hold for them, or for entering upon the university course which some had chosen. Mr. Winterhalter gave them some very earnest words at the close, and some grateful ones, too, as if he felt that the favors had not all been on one side. Then the crowd went away, and the First Class's school days were over.

There was a quiet reunion that evening in Mr. Winterhalter's parlor, where the graduating class gathered, and old pupils and young met together. All too quickly the evening passed, and when the room began to get a little thinned and there was a constant flitting away, after many " good nights " and much hand-shaking, Gilbert, who was talking with Payne, an old graduate of the school, felt some one pulling at his sleeve. Turning, he saw Tom Fowler, who said, " I know it's horridly impolite, but I can't help it. I 've come to say good by."

" Why," said Gilbert, " you don't go to-night ? "

" Oh, no ; but I go at five to-morrow morning,— before daylight, and before you 'll be up. I have to take the earliest train in order to get home the same day, and to-morrow is Saturday, you know."

Mr. Payne, having been a school-boy himself, knew what would be most agreeable to the two, and moved away — to Tom's great delight — saying, " We 'll finish that discussion by and by, Starr."

" I oughtn't to 've interrupted you, I know," said Tom, apologetically, drawing Gilbert into the silence and shadow of a curtained window ; " but what is a fellow to

do ? and how can he stand on ceremony the
last day? I've got a better right to you
than Payne."

"I don't dispute that," said Gilbert, cor-
dially; "and I'm sorry that you aren't going
to stay till to-morrow night — till the rest of
us go."

"So am I; but it can't be. Now I might
as well out with what I've got to say, for
this evening is about over. What do you
think I did last night, captain? — after we
got back from the race."

"I'm sure I can't tell," said Gilbert, per-
ceiving that Tom looked very earnest about
something.

"Well, I did that which I didn't want
to go away without telling you of. The
thought of doing it has been hanging upon
me ever since I got well of the fever, but it
wasn't till last night that I got courage
enough to go about it. I marched straight

in to Mr. Winterhalter — I suppose I went through with it like a pedler getting off the list of his goods, for the kind old fellow looked smilish all about his eyes — and says I, 'Mr. Winterhalter, I'm a cheat!' 'I know it,' said he. That rather staggered me, but screwing up my courage I managed to get out, 'And I'm ashamed and sorry and cut-up about it, and I'd like you to forgive me if it *is* the last minute. I feel dreadful small, sir.' I can tell you I *did*, too! The good old fellow was silent a minute, think-ing, I suppose, and then he said, in these very words that fairly upset me — 'Tom, I know all about the deception that won the flag last summer; but Gilbert Starr took all the blame for that act a year ago. So I have nothing to say about the matter.' If he had got up and knocked me down I shouldn't have minded it half so much as those words. I stood there as dumb as that mummy in our museum, and he must have took pity upon me, for said he, taking my hand, 'Tom, you did right to come' to me about this. I think I understand you, and I'm sure I forgive you; go and talk with Gilbert about it.' Then he looked right through me with his keen eyes and sent me off; and this is the first chance I've got at you."

Tom stopped, and looked steadfastly at Gilbert. The captain had parted the curtain and was looking out into the starry, silent night, and Tom fancied — nay, was quite certain — that his chin trembled and his mouth quivered a little, though why they should do so was beyond Tom's comprehension.

" Say," said he, energetically, " don't look away from me in that style. What have I said? What are you blue about?"

" *Blue!* " said Gilbert, turning back to his

friend. "I'm happy! — more than I can tell."

"So am I," said Ray, who came up in time to hear the last of Gilbert's exclamation.

"Pshaw! go away, Hunter," cried Tom. "You're to have him all to yourself the rest of the month, besides going through college with him, and now I want the captain to myself a minute longer."

Ray went away.

"Now," said Tom, "keep your patience just a minute longer and I'm done. If a fellow should treat you well all the time that you were treating him shamefully — if he should take care of you through a deathly fever and take his pay in a long sickness, with compound interest, too, and then if he should just smother you entirely by getting well and treating you as if you were his brother, and fairly annihilate you with the lesson he teaches, presses home and crowds down without any letting up, how would you feel toward this fellow?"

"Well," said Gilbert, laughing, "I'm afraid I should feel as if he had rather over-burdened me."

"No, you wouldn't!—not if all this came little by little, as it came to me. You'd bless the day that ever you knew this fellow!—just as I do," said Tom, with a slight tremor in his voice.

They were silent a few minutes, the gay and merry chatter of the company floating out to them. Then Tom said, with an effort, "I *must* go,—I haven't packed yet. If ever I can make up my mind to a college, I—I'll come where you are. And now—how can I say it?—Good by, captain."

"Good by, Tom."

Then Tom drew his hand from Gilbert's and walked straight to the parlor-door, looking neither to the right nor left.

Then Ray, who had been hovering near, came up and said, " I 'm glad I haven't got to go through what poor Tom did just now. Am I not a lucky fellow? But you 're not to stay here any longer, for Mr. Payne is waiting for you. Come along ! "

Gilbert followed his friend and spent the remainder of the evening in the busiest of chat; and when he awoke the next morning, Tom was gone. But on the bed, scrawled over a great piece of paper, was this:

" *Four o'clock in the morning.*
Good by, once more, Cap, and don't forget
ToM FOWLER."

Gilbert and Ray, as well as most of the class, were busy enough all the forenoon in picking up books and papers and packing their trunks. After dinner, when the trunks and boxes had been got off to the depot, they took a hurried ramble over all the pleasant haunts that seven happy years had made dear, and returned to be astonished at finding that it was actually three o'clock.

"Ah," said Gilbert, "only two more hours! We must go to the study next, Ray."

They found Mrs. Winterhalter there, and alone. Ray had something to say to the good lady, and Gilbert had time to look around at the familiar book-cases, the great easy-chairs, the little work-table and the pictures on the wall — each and all of them associated with so many different events in his life — and, sitting here, he wondered if there was another spot in the wide earth that could ever seem so dear and home-like.

In the midst of his reverie, Ray stepped out, thinking, "I'll just give good Mrs. Winterhalter a chance to say what she likes to Gil, while I get our valise and the overcoats ready. He'll stay till the last minute I'll warrant."

And presently Gilbert was astonished to find his friend gone and Mrs. Winterhalter bending over her work with a grave face.

" Gilbert," said she, in the gentle tone that was so pleasant to his ears, and just as if she had divined his thoughts, " doesn't this seem like home to you ? "

" Yes — you don't know — I can't tell you how much like home, Mrs. Winterhalter," he said; " and it *is* home, — I've been here so long."

" Yes," she said, musingly, " longer, much longer than any of the others. You were a little boy when you came here. That is the way with Mr. Winterhalter and I — our boys grow up to men, and when they have got to be like our own, we have to say farewell and let them go. Some of them come back once in a great while, but most of them — ah, it's like saying good by forever when they go."

"But it will not be so with me," said Gilbert, quickly and eagerly. "I shall come again often — if you 'll let me. It's home ! "

"I'm glad to hear you say that," said Mrs. Winterhalter. "We shall look for you at your vacation, we shall be proud of your successes, we shall be glad and happy to find that you are our own Gilbert Starr still, and that your feet keep in the path which you have chosen since coming to live with us. Seven years ! why, every one of them has been making you our boy." The good lady laid down her work.

Gilbert wanted to add, "And every one of them has been making you like a mother to me," but the words did not leave his tongue ; though they might have done if Mr. Winterhalter had not entered just then.

"Ah, Gilbert," said he, warmly, putting out both his hands, "how are we going to part with you ? School will not be school, now; we shall miss you in everything. But though poor Mrs. Winterhalter and I have to lose our boys once in so often, this seems another matter. You are our own; we watched you, and were glad when you were glad, and happy when you were happy, and now —" Here Mr. Winterhalter stopped; why, it was not evident, unless he had suddenly lost his voice. But he filled up the blank by shaking both of Gilbert's hands very heartily; and here Ray came tapping at the study-door and calling, " Gilbert !"

Mrs. Winterhalter looked up at the clock, and trying to keep her face bright and cheery, said, " Well, it will not be so hard if we know we can have you back again; and when may I expect to hear your step in the hall, and your tap at the door, and you saying, ' Mrs. Winterhalter !'"

The good lady's voice got tremulous at the last, and the husband was fain to say, " Let it be soon, Gilbert."

"It shall be!" said Gilbert, getting up just as another impatient " *Gilbert!* " came from without the door. " I 'll come back to you — I shall want to come. How can I forget ? "

His two friends followed him to the door. " God bless you ! " said Mrs. Winterhalter, laying her soft hand upon his head, " and may He keep our boy." And with her words thrilling him, Gilbert bent and kissed her hand, and passed out of the dear portal — along the piazza, and down the steps, with eyes that could see nothing clearly for the tears that were in them. But at the gate he stopped to look back.

" Twenty minutes past five," said Ray, leaning against a tree-trunk and looking at his watch ; " just ten minutes left in which to get to the depot." But Gilbert did not heed.

The westering sun lit up the great, many-angled building, and touched the lawn-side and the garden goldenly, and never were they fairer in the eyes of the gazer at the gate. The blessed picture, in those few seconds, painted itself upon his heart; and the warm breath of wind, the rustle of the grass, the faint sigh of the river far below, all seemed to whisper of other days, and a little figure, and yet—not at all of sorrow or sadness.

" Gilbert ! " said Ray, in a desperate voice. And then he turned away.